P.H.

THE KANSAS QUESTION.

E
445
.K2
S95

SENATOR SUMNER'S SPEECH,

Reviewing the Action of the Federal Administration upon the

SUBJECT OF SLAVERY IN KANSAS;

DELIVERED IN THE SENATE OF THE UNITED STATES,

May 19th and 20th, 1856.

CINCINNATI:
PUBLISHED BY GEO. S. BLANCHARD, 39 WEST FOURTH STREET.
1856.

Copies sent by mail, on receipt of Six cents in postage stamps. Five Dollars per 100.

Gift
Prof. H. L. Wilgus
1-8-34

SPEECH OF HON. CHARLES SUMNER.

Mr. President:

You are now called to redress a great transgression. Seldom in the history of nations has such a question been presented. Tariffs, army bills, navy bills, land bills, are important, and justly occupy your care; but these all belong to the course of ordinary legislation. As means and instruments only, they are necessarily subordinate to the conservation of Government itself. Grant them or deny them, in greater or less degree, and you will inflict no shock. The machinery of Government will continue to move. The State will not cease to exist. Far otherwise is it with the eminent question now before you, involving, as it does, Liberty in a broad Territory, and also involving the peace of the whole country with our good name in history forevermore.

Take down your map, sir, and you will find that the Territory of Kansas, more than any other region, occupies the middle spot of North America, equally distant from the Atlantic on the east, and the Pacific on the west; from the frozen waters of Hudson's Bay on the north, and the tepid Gulf Stream on the south, constituting the precise territorial centre of the whole vast Continent. To such advantages of situation, on the very highway between two oceans, are added a soil of unsurpassed richness, and a fascinating, undulating beauty of surface, with a health-giving climate, calculated to nurture a powerful and generous people, worthy to be a central pivot of American Institutions. A few short months only have passed since this spacious mediterranean country was open only to the savage, who ran wild in its woods and prairies; and now it has already drawn to its bosom a population of freemen larger than Athens crowded within her historic gates, when her sons, under Miltiades, won Liberty for mankind on the field of Marathon; more than Sparta contained when she ruled Greece, and sent forth her devoted children, quickened by a mother's benediction, to return with their shields or on them; more than Rome gathered on her seven hills, when, under her kings, she commenced that sovereign sway, which afterwards embraced the whole earth; more than London held, when, on the fields of Crecy and Agincourt, the English banner was carried victoriously over the chivalrous hosts of France.

Against this Territory, thus fortunate in position and population, a Crime has been committed, which is without example in the records of the Past. Not in plundered provinces or in the cruelties of selfish governors will you find its parallel; and yet there is an ancient instance, which may show at least the path of justice. In the terrible impeachment by which the great Roman Orator has blasted through all time the name of Verres, amidst charges of robbery and sacrilege, the enormity which most aroused the indignant voice of his accuser, and which still stands forth with strongest distinctness, arresting the sympathetic indignation of all who read the story, is, that away in Sicily he had scourged a citizen of Rome—that the cry "I am a Roman citizen" had been interposed in vain against the lash of the tyrant governor. Other charges were, that he had carried away productions of art, and that he had violated the sacred shrines. It was in the presence of the Roman Senate that this arraignment proceeded; in a temple of the Forum; amidst crowds—such as no orator had ever before drawn together—thronging the porticos and colonnades, even clinging to the house tops and neighboring slopes—and under the anxious gaze of witnesses summoned from the scene of crime. But an audience grander far—of higher dignity—of more various people and of wider intelligence—the countless multitude of succeeding generations, in every land, where eloquence has been studied or where the Roman name has been recognised—has listened to the accusation, and throbbed with condemnation of the criminal. Sir, speaking in an age of light and in a land of constitutional liberty, where the safeguards of elections are justly placed among the highest triumphs of civilization, I fearlessly assert that the wrongs of much-abused Sicily, thus memorable in history, were small by the side of the wrongs of Kansas, where the very shrines of popular institutions, more sacred than any heathen altar, have been desecrated; where the ballot-box, more precious than any work, in ivory or marble, from the cunning hand of art, has been plundered; and where the cry "I am an American citizen" has been interposed in vain against outrage of every kind, even upon life itself. Are you against sacrilege? I present it for your execration. Are you against robbery? I hold it up to your scorn. Are you for the protection of

American citizens? I show you how their dearest rights have been cloven down, while a Tyrannical Usurpation has sought to install itself on their very necks!

But the wickedness which I now begin to expose is immeasurably aggravated by the motive which prompted it. Not in any common lust for power did this uncommon tragedy have its origin. It is the rape of a virgin Territory, compelling it to the hateful embrace of Slavery; and it may be clearly traced to a depraved longing for a new slave State, the hideous offspring of such a crime, in the hope of adding to the power of Slavery in the National Government. Yes, sir, when the whole world, alike Christian and Turk, is rising up to condemn this wrong, and to make it a hissing to the nations, here in our Republic, *force*—aye, sir, FORCE—has been openly employed in compelling Kansas to this pollution, and all for the sake of political power. There is the simple fact, which you will vainly attempt to deny, but which in itself presents an essential wickedness that makes other public crimes seem like public virtues.

But this enormity, vast beyond comparison, swells to dimensions of wickedness which the imagination toils in vain to grasp, when it is understood, that for this purpose are hazarded the horrors of intestine feud, not only in this distant Territory, but everywhere throughout the country. Already the muster has begun. The strife is no longer local, but national. Even now, while I speak, portents hang on all the arches of the horizon, threatening to darken the broad land, which already yawns with the mutterings of civil war. The fury of the propagandists of Slavery, and the calm determination of their opponents, are now diffused from the distant Territory over wide-spread communities, and the whole country, in all its extent—marshalling hostile divisions, and foreshadowing a strife, which, unless happily averted by the triumph of Freedom, will become war — fratricidal, parricidal war — with an accumulated wickedness beyond the wickedness of any war in human annals; justly provoking the avenging judgment of Providence and the avenging pen of history, and constituting a strife, in the language of the ancient writer, more than *foreign*, more than *social*, more than *civil*; but something compounded of all these strifes, and in itself more than war; *sed potius commune quoddam ex omnibus, et plus quam bellum.*

Such is the Crime which you are to judge. But the criminal also must be dragged into day, that you may see and measure the power by which all this wrong is sustained. From no common source could it proceed. In its perpetration, was needed a spirit of vaulting ambition which would hesitate at nothing; a hardihood of purpose which was insensible to the judgment of mankind; a madness for Slavery which should disregard the Constitution, the laws, and all the great examples of our history; also a consciousness of power such as comes from the habit of power; a combination of energies found only in a hundred arms directed by a hundred eyes; a control of Public Opinion, through venal pens and a prostituted press; an ability to subsidize crowds in every vocation of life—the politician with his local importance, the lawyer with his subtle tongue, and even the authority of the judge on the bench; and a familiar use of men in places high and low, so that none, from the President to the lowest border postmaster, should decline to be its tool; all these things and more were needed; and they were found in the Slave Power of our Republic. There, sir, stands the criminal—all unmasked before you—heartless, grasping, and tyrannical—with an audacity beyond that of Verres, a subtlety beyond that of Machiavel, a meanness beyond that of Bacon, and an ability beyond that of Hastings. Justice to Kansas can be secured only by the prostration of this influence; for this is the Power behind—greater than any President—which succors and sustains the Crime. Nay, the proceedings I now arraign derive their fearful consequence only from this connection.

In now opening this great matter, I am not insensible to the austere demands of the occasion; but the dependence of the crime against Kansas upon the Slave Power is so peculiar and important, that I trust to be pardoned while I impress it by an illustration, which to some may seem trivial. It is related in Northern mythology, that the god of Force, visiting an enchanted region, was challenged by his royal entertainer to what seemed a humble feat of strength—merely, sir, to lift a cat from the ground. The god smiled at the challenge, and, calmly placing his hand under the belly of the animal, with superhuman strength, strove, while the back of the feline monster arched far upwards, even beyond reach, and one paw actually forsook the earth, until at last the discomfited divinity desisted; but he was little surprised at his defeat, when he learned that this créature, which seemed to be a cat, and nothing more, was not merely a cat, but that it belonged to and was a part of the great Terrestrial Serpent, which, in its innumerable folds, encircled the whole globe. Even so the creature, whose paws are now fastened upon Kansas, whatever it may seem to be, constitutes in reality a part of the Slave Power, which, with loathsome folds, is now coiled about the whole land. Thus do I expose the extent of the present contest, where we encounter not merely local resistance, but also the unconquered sustaining arm behind. But out of the vastness of the Crime attempted, with all its woe and shame, I derive a well-founded assurance of a commensurate vastness of effort against it, by the aroused masses of the country, determined not only to vindicate Right against Wrong, but to redeem the Republic from the thraldom of that Oligarchy, which prompts, directs, and concentrates, the distant wrong.

Such is the Crime, and such the criminal, which it is my duty in this debate to expose, and, by the blessing of God, this duty shall be done completely to the end. But this will not be enough. The Apologies, which, with strange hardihood, have been offered for the Crime, must be torn away, so that it shall stand forth, without a single rag, or fig-leaf, to cover its vileness. And, finally, the True Remedy must be shown. The subject is complex in its relations, as it is transcendent in importance; and yet, if I am honored by your attention, I hope to exhibit it clearly in all its parts, while I conduct you to the inevitable conclusion, that Kansas must be admitted at once, with her present Constitution, as a State of this Union, and give a new star to the blue field of our National Flag. And here I derive satisfaction from the thought, that the cause is so strong in itself as to bear even the infirmities of its advocates; nor can it require anything beyond that simplicity of treatment and moderation of manner which I desire to cultivate. Its true character is such, that, like Hercules, it will conquer just so soon as it is recognised.

My task will be divided under three different heads; *first*, THE CRIME AGAINST KANSAS, in its origin and extent; *secondly*, THE APOLOGIES FOR THE CRIME; and *thirdly*, the TRUE REMEDY.

But, before entering upon the argument, I must say something of a general character, particularly in response to what has fallen from Senators who have raised themselves to eminence on this floor in championship of human wrongs; I mean the Senator from South Carolina, [Mr. BUTLER,] and the Senator from Illinois, [Mr. DOUGLAS,] who, though unlike as Don Quixote and Sancho Panza, yet, like this couple, sally forth together in the same adventure. I regret much to miss the elder Senator from his seat; but the cause, against which he has run a tilt, with such activity of animosity, demands that the opportunity of exposing him should not be lost; and it is for the cause that I speak. The Senator from South Carolina has read many books of chivalry, and believes himself a chivalrous knight, with sentiments of honor and courage. Of course he has chosen a mistress to whom he has made his vows, and who, though ugly to others, is always lovely to him; though polluted in the sight of the world, is chaste in his sight—I mean the harlot, Slavery. For her, his tongue is always profuse in words. Let her be impeached in character, or any proposition made to shut her out from the extension of her wantonness, and no extravagance of manner or hardihood of assertion is then too great for this Senator. The frenzy of Don Quixote, in behalf of his wench Dulcinea del Toboso, is all surpassed. The asserted rights of Slavery, which shock equality of all kinds, are cloaked by a fantastic claim of equality. If the slave States cannot enjoy what, in mockery of the great fathers of the Republic, he misnames equality under the Constitution—in other words, the full power in the National Territories to compel fellow-men to unpaid toil, to separate husband and wife, and to sell little children at the auction block—then, sir, the chivalric Senator will conduct the State of South Carolina out of the Union! Heroic knight! Exalted Senator! A second Moses come for a second exodus!

But not content with this poor menace, which we have been twice told was "measured," the Senator, in the unrestrained chivalry of his nature, has undertaken to apply opprobrious words to those who differ from him on this floor. He calls them "sectional and fanatical;" and opposition to the usurpation in Kansas, he denounces as "an uncalculating fanaticism." To be sure, these charges lack all grace of originality, and all sentiment of truth; but the adventurous Senator does not hesitate. He is the uncompromising, unblushing representative on this floor of a flagrant *sectionalism*, which now domineers over the Republic, and yet with a ludicrous ignorance of his own position—unable to see himself as others see him—or with an effrontery which even his white head ought not to protect from rebuke, he applies to those here who resist his *sectionalism* the very epithet which designates himself. The men who strive to bring back the Government to its original policy, when Freedom and not Slavery was national, while Slavery and not Freedom was sectional, he arraigns as *sectional*. This will not do. It involves too great a perversion of terms. I tell that Senator, that it is to himself, and to the "organization" of which he is the "committed advocate," that this epithet belongs. I now fasten it upon them. For myself, I care little for names; but since the question has been raised here, I affirm that the Republican party of the Union is in no just sense *sectional*, but, more than any other party, *national;* and that it now goes forth to dislodge from the high places of the Government the tyrannical sectionalism of which the Senator from South Carolina is one of the maddest zealots.

To the charge of fanaticism I also reply. Sir, fanaticism is found in an enthusiasm or exaggeration of opinions, particularly on religious subjects; but there may be a fanaticism for evil as well as for good. Now, I will not deny, that there are persons among us loving Liberty too well for their personal good, in a selfish generation. Such there may be, and, for the sake of their example, would that there were more! In calling them "fanatics," you cast contumely upon the noble army of martyrs, from the earliest day down to this hour; upon the great tribunes of human rights, by whom life, liberty, and happiness, on earth, have been secured; upon the long line of devoted patriots, who, throughout history, have truly loved their country; and, upon all, who, in noble aspirations for the general good and in forgetfulness of self, have stood out before their age, and gathered into their generous bosoms the shafts of tyranny and wrong, in order to make a pathway for Truth. You discredit Luther, when alone he nailed his articles to the door of the church at Wittenberg, and then, to the imperial demand that he should retract, firmly replied, "Here I stand; I cannot do otherwise, so help me God!" You discredit Hampden, when alone he refused to pay the few shillings of ship-money, and shook the throne of Charles I; you discredit Milton, when, amidst the corruptions of a heartless Court, he lived on, the lofty friend of Liberty, above question or suspicion; you discredit Russell and Sidney, when, for the sake of their country, they calmly turned from family and friends, to tread the narrow steps of the scaffold; you discredit those early founders of American institutions, who preferred the hardships of a wilderness, surrounded by a savage foe, to injustice on beds of ease; you discredit our later fathers, who, few in numbers and weak in resources, yet strong in their cause, did not hesitate to brave the mighty power of England, already encircling the globe with her morning drum-beats. Yes, sir, of such are the fanatics of history, according to the Senator. But I tell that Senator, that there are characters badly eminent, of whose fanaticism there can be no question. Such were the ancient Egyptians, who worshipped divinities in brutish forms; the Druids, who darkened the forests of oak, in which they lived, by sacrifices of blood; the Mexicans, who surrendered countless victims to the propitiation of their obscene idols; the Spaniards, who, under Alva, sought to force the Inquisition upon Holland, by a tyranny kindred to that now employed to force Slavery upon Kansas; and such were the Algerines, when in solemn conclave, after listening to a speech not unlike that of the Senator from South Carolina, they resolved to continue the slavery of white Christians, and to extend it to the countrymen of Washington! Aye, sir, extend it! And in this same dreary catalogue faithful history must record all who now, in an enlightened age and in a land of boasted Freedom, stand up, in perversion of the Constitution and in denial of immortal truth, to fasten a new shackle upon their fellow-man. If the Senator wishes to see fanatics, let him look round among his own associates; let him look at himself.

But I have not done with the Senator. There is another matter regarded by him of such consequence, that he interpolated it into the speech of the Senator from New Hampshire, [MR. HALE,] and also announced that he had prepared himself with it, to take in his pocket all the way to Boston, when he expected to address the people of that community. On this account, and for the sake of truth, I stop for one moment, and tread it to the earth. The North, according to the Senator, was engaged in the slave trade, and helped to introduce slaves into the Southern States; and this undeniable fact he proposed to establish by statistics, in stating which his errors surpassed his sentences in number. But I let these pass for the present, that I may deal with his argument. Pray, sir, is the acknowledged turpitude of a departed generation to become an example for us? And yet the suggestion of the Senator, if entitled to any consideration in this discussion, must have this extent. I join my friend from New Hampshire in thanking the Senator from South Carolina for adducing this instance; for it gives me an opportunity to say, that the Northern merchants, with homes in Boston, Bristol, Newport, New York, and Philadelphia, who catered for Slavery during the years of the slave trade, are the lineal progenitors of the Northern men, with homes in these places, who lend themselves to Slavery in our day; and especially that all, whether North or South, who take part, directly or indirectly, in the conspiracy against Kansas, do but continue the work of the slave-traders, which you condemn. It is true, too true, alas! that our fathers were engaged in this traffic; but that is no apology for it. And in repelling the authority of this example, I repel also the trite argument founded on the earlier example of England. It is true that our mother country, at the peace of Utrecht, extorted from Spain the Assiento Contract, securing the monopoly of the slave trade with the Spanish Colonies, as the whole price of all the blood of great victories; that she higgled at Aix-la-Chapelle for another lease of this exclusive traffic; and again, at the treaty of Madrid, clung to the wretched piracy. It is true, that in this spirit the power of the mother country was prostituted to the same base ends in her American Colonies, against indignant protests from our fathers. All these things now rise up in judgment against her. Let us not follow the Senator from South Carolina to do the very evil to-day, which in another generation we condemn.

As the Senator from South Carolina is the Don Quixote, the Senator from Illinois [MR. DOUGLAS] is the squire of Slavery, its very Sancho Panza, ready to do all its humiliating offices. This Senator, in his labored address, vindicating his labored report—piling one mass of elaborate error upon another mass—constrained himself, as you will remember, to unfamiliar decencies of speech. Of that address I have nothing to say at this moment, though before I sit down I shall show something of its fallacies. But I go back now to an earlier occasion, when, true to his native impulses, he threw into this discussion, "for a charm of powerful trouble," personalities most discreditable to this body. I will not stop to repel the imputations which he cast upon myself; but I mention them to remind you of the "sweltered venom sleeping got," which, with other poisoned ingredients, he cast into the cauldron of this debate. Of other things I speak. Standing on this floor, the Senator issued his rescript, requiring submission to the Usurped Power of Kansas; and this was accompanied by a manner—all his own—such as befits the tyrannical threat. Very well. Let the Senator try. I tell him now that he cannot enforce any such submission. The Senator, with the Slave Power at his back, is strong; but he is not strong enough for this purpose. He is bold. He shrinks from nothing. Like Danton, he may cry, "*l'audace! l'audace! toujours l'audace!*" but even his audacity cannot compass this work. The Senator copies the British officer, who, with boastful swagger, said that with the hilt of his sword he would cram the "stamps" down the throats of the American people, and he will meet a similar failure. He may convulse this country with civil feud. Like the ancient madman, he may set fire to this Temple of Constitutional Liberty, grander than Ephesian dome; but he cannot enforce obedience to that tyrannical Usurpation.

The Senator dreams that he can subdue the North. He disclaims the open threat, but his conduct still implies it. How little that Senator knows himself, or the strength of the cause which he persecutes! He is but a mortal man; against him is an immortal principle. With finite power he wrestles with the infinite, and he must fall. Against him are stronger battalions than any marshalled by mortal arm—the inborn, ineradicable, invincible sentiments of the human heart; against him is nature in all her subtle forces; against him is God. Let him try to subdue these.

But I pass from these things, which, though belonging to the very heart of the discussion, are yet preliminary in character, and press at once to the main question.

I. It belongs to me now, in the first place, to expose the CRIME AGAINST KANSAS, in its origin and extent. Logically, this is the beginning of the argument. I say Crime, and deliberately adopt this strongest term, as better than any other denoting the consummate transgression. I would go further, if language could further go. It is the *Crime of Crimes*—surpassing far the old *crimen majestatis*, pursued with vengeance by the laws of Rome, and containing all other crimes, as the greater contains the less. I do not go too far, when I call it the *Crime against Nature*, from which the soul recoils, and which language refuses to describe. To lay bare this enormity, I now proceed. The whole subject has already become a twice-told tale, and its renewed recital will be a renewal of its sorrow and shame; but I shall not hesitate to enter upon it. The occasion requires it from the beginning.

It has been well remarked by a distinguished historian of our country, that, at the Ithuriel touch of the Missouri discussion, the slave interest, hitherto hardly recognised as a distinct element in our system, started up portentous and dilated, with threats and assumptions, which are the origin of our existing national politics. This was in 1820. The discussion ended with the admission of Missouri as a slaveholding State, and the prohibition of Slavery in all the remaining territory west of the Mississippi, and north of 36° 30′, leaving the condition of other territory south of this line, or subsequently acquired, untouched by the arrangement. Here was a solemn act of legislation, called at the time a compromise, a covenant, a compact, first brought forward in this body by a slaveholder—vindicated by slaveholders in debate—finally sanctioned by slaveholding votes—also upheld at the time by the essential approbation of a slaveholding President, James Monroe, and his Cabinet, of whom a majority were slaveholders, including Mr. Calhoun himself; and this compromise was made the condition of the admission of Missouri, without which that State could not have been received into the Union. The bargain was simple, and was applicable, of course, only to the territory named. Leaving all other territory to await the judgment of another generation, the South said to the North, Conquer your prejudices so far as to admit Missouri as a slave State, and, in consideration of this much-coveted boon, Slavery shall be prohibited forever in all the remaining Louisiana Territory above 36° 30′; and the North yielded.

In total disregard of history, the President, in his annual message, has told us that this compromise "was *reluctantly* acquiesced in by the Southern States." Just the contrary is true. It was the work of slaveholders, and was crowded by their concurring votes upon a reluctant North. At the time it was hailed by slaveholders as a victory. Charles Pinckney, of South Carolina, in an oft-quoted letter, written at three o'clock on the night of its passage, says, "It is considered here by the slaveholding States as a great triumph." At the North it was accepted as a defeat, and the friends of Freedom everywhere throughout the country bowed their heads with mortification. But little did they know the completeness of their disaster. Little did they dream that the prohibition of Slavery in the Territory, which was stipulated as the price of their fatal capitulation, would also at the very moment of its maturity be wrested from them.

Time passed, and it became necessary to provide for this Territory an organized Government. Suddenly, without notice in the public press, or the prayer of a single petition, or one word of open recommendation from the President—after an acquiescence of thirty-three years, and the irreclaimable possession by the South of its special share under this compromise—in violation of every obligation of honor, compact, and good neighborhood—and in contemptuous disregard of the out-gushing sentiments of an aroused North, this time-honored prohibition, in itself a Landmark of Freedom, was overturned, and the vast region now known as Kansas and Nebraska was opened to Slavery. It was natural that a measure thus repugnant in character should be pressed by arguments mutually repugnant. It was urged on two principal reasons, so opposite and inconsistent as to slap each other in the face—one being that, by the repeal of the prohibition, the Territory would be left open to the entry of slaveholders with their slaves, without hindrance; and the other being, that the people would be left absolutely free to determine the question for themselves, and to prohibit the entry of slaveholders with their slaves, if they should think best. With some, the apology was the alleged rights of slaveholders; with others, it was the alleged rights of the people. With some, it was openly the extension of Slavery; and with others, it was openly the establishment of Freedom, under the guise of Popular Sovereignty. Of course, the measure, thus upheld in defiance of reason, was carried through Congress in defiance of all the securities of legislation; and I mention these things that you may see in what foulness the present Crime was engendered.

It was carried, *first*, by *whipping in* to its support, through Executive influence and patronage, men who acted against their own declared judgment and the known will of their constituents. *Secondly*, by *foisting out of place*, both in the Senate and House of Representatives, important business, long pending, and usurping its room. *Thirdly*, by *trampling under foot* the rules of the House of Representatives, always before the safeguard of the minority. And *fourthly*, by *driving it to a close* during the very session in which it originated, so that it might not be arrested by the indignant voice of the People. Such are some of the means by which this snap judgment was obtained. If the clear will of the People had not been disregarded, it could not have passed. If the Government had not nefariously interposed its influence, it could not have passed. If it had been left to its natural place in the order of business, it could not have passed. If the rules of the House and the rights of the minority had not been violated, it could not have passed. If it had been allowed to go over to another Congress, when the People might be heard, it would have been ended; and then the Crime we now deplore, would have been without its first seminal life.

Mr. President, I mean to keep absolutely within the limits of parliamentary propriety. I make no personal imputations; but only with frankness, such as belongs to the occasion and my own character, describe a great historical act, which is now enrolled in the Capitol. Sir, the Nebraska Bill was in every respect a swindle. It was a swindle by the South of the North. It was, on the part of those who had already completely enjoyed their share of the Missouri Compromise, a swindle of those whose share was yet absolutely untouched; and the plea of unconstitutionality set up—like the plea of usury after the borrowed money has been enjoyed—did not make it less a swindle. Urged as a Bill of Peace, it was a swindle of the whole country. Urged as opening the doors to slave-masters with their slaves, it was a swindle of the asserted doctrine of Popular Sovereignty. Urged as sanctioning Popular Sovereignty, it was a swindle of the asserted rights of slave-masters. It was a swindle of a broad territory, thus cheated of protection against Slavery. It was a swindle of a great cause, early espoused by Washington, Franklin, and Jefferson, surrounded by the best fathers of the Republic. Sir, it was a swindle of God-given inalienable Rights. Turn it over; look at it on all sides, and it is everywhere a swindle; and, if the word I now employ has not the authority of classical usage, it has, on this occasion, the indubitable authority of fitness. No other word will adequately express the mingled meanness and wickedness of the cheat.

Its character was still further apparent in the general structure of the bill. Amidst overflowing professions of regard for the sovereignty of the people in the Territory, they were despoiled of every essential privilege of sovereignty. They were not allowed to choose their Governor, Secretary, Chief Justice, Associate Justices, Attorney, or Marshal—all of whom are sent from Washington; nor were they allowed to regulate the salaries of any of these functionaries, or the daily allowance of the legislative body, or even the pay of the clerks and doorkeepers; but [illegible]e left free to adopt Slavery. And this w[illegible] Popular Sovereignty! Time does not allo[illegible] does the occasion require, that I should s[illegible] to dwell on this transparent device to cover a transcendent wrong. Suffice it to say, that Slavery is in itself an arrogant denial of Human Rights, and by no human reason can the power to establish such a wrong be placed among the attributes of any [illegible]ust sovereignty. In refusing it such a place, I do not deny popular rights, but uphold them; I do not restrain popular rights, but extend them. And, sir, to this conclusion you must yet come, unless deaf, not only to the admonitions of political justice, but also to the genius of our own Constitution, under which, when properly interpreted, no valid claim for Slavery can be set up anywhere in the National territory. The Senator from Michigan [Mr. CASS] may say, in response to the Senator from Mississippi, [Mr. BROWN,] that Slavery cannot go into the Territory under the Constitution, without legislative introduction; and permit me to add, in response to both, that Slavery cannot go there at all. *Nothing can come out of nothing;* and there is absolutely nothing in the Constitution out of which Slavery can be derived, while there are provisions, which, when properly interpreted, make its existence anywhere within the exclusive National jurisdiction impossible.

The offensive provision in the bill was in its form a legislative anomaly, utterly wanting the natural directness and simplicity of an honest transaction. It did not undertake openly to repeal the old Prohibition of Slavery, but seemed to mince the matter, as if conscious of the swindle. It said that this Prohibition, "being inconsistent with the principle of non-intervention by Congress with Slavery in the States and Territories, as recognised by the legislation of 1850, commonly called the Compromise Measures, is hereby declared inoperative and void." Thus, with insidious ostentation, was it pretended that an act, violating the greatest compromise of our legislative history, and setting loose the foundations of all compromise, was derived out of a compromise. Then followed in the Bill the further declaration, which is entirely without precedent, and which has been aptly called "a stump speech in its belly," namely: "it being the true intent and meaning of this act, not to legislate Slavery into any Territory or State, nor to exclude it therefrom, but to leave the people thereof perfectly free to form and regulate their domestic institutions in their own way, subject only to the Constitution of the United States." Here were smooth words, such as belong to a cunning tongue enlisted in a bad cause. But whatever may have been their various hidden meanings, this at least was evident, that, by their effect, the Congressional Prohibition of Slavery, which had always been regarded as a seven-fold shield, covering the whole Louisiana Territory north of 36° 30′, was now removed, while a principle was declared, which would render the supplementary Prohibition of Slavery in Minnesota, Oregon, and Washington, "inoperative and void," and thus open to Slavery all these vast regions, now the rude cradles of mighty States. Here you see the magnitude of the mischief contemplated. But my purpose now is with the Crime against Kansas, and I shall not stop to expose the conspiracy beyond.

Mr. President, men are wisely presumed to intend the natural consequences of their conduct, and to seek what their acts seem to promote. Now, the Nebraska Bill, on its very face, openly cleared the way for Slavery, and it is not wrong to presume that its originators intended the natural consequences of such an act, and sought in this way to extend Slavery. Of course, they did. And this is the first stage in the Crime against Kansas.

But this was speedily followed by other developments. The bare-faced scheme was soon whispered, that Kansas must be a slave State. In conformity with this idea was the Government of this unhappy Territory organized in all its departments; and thus did the President, by whose complicity the Prohibition of Slavery had been overthrown, lend himself to a new complicity—giving to the conspirators a lease of connivance, amounting even to copartnership. The Governor, Secretary, Chief Justice, Associate Justices, Attorney, and Marshal, with a whole caucus of other stipendiaries, nominated by the President and confirmed by the Senate, were all commended as friendly to Slavery. No man, with the sentiments of Washington, or Jefferson, or Franklin, found any favor; nor is it too much to say, that, had these great patriots once more come among us, not one of them, with his recorded unretracted opinions on Slavery, could have been nominated by the President or confirmed by the Senate for any post in that Territory. With such auspices the conspiracy proceeded. Even in advance of the Nebraska Bill, secret societies were organized in Missouri, ostensibly to protect her institutions, and afterwards, under the name of "Self-Defensive Associations," and of "Blue Lodges," these were multiplied throughout the western counties of that State, *before any counter-movement from the North.* It was confidently anticipated, that, by the activity of these societies, and the interest of slaveholders everywhere, with the advantage derived from the neighborhood of Missouri, and the influence of the Territorial Government, Slavery might be introduced into Kansas, quietly but surely, without arousing a conflict—that the crocodile egg might be stealthily dropped in the sun-burnt soil, there to be hatched unobserved until it sent forth its reptile monster.

But the conspiracy was unexpectedly balked. The debate, which convulsed Congress, had stirred the whole country. Attention from all sides was directed upon Kansas, which at once became the favorite goal of emigration. The Bill had loudly declared, that its object was "to leave the people perfectly free to form and regulate their domestic institutions in their own way;" and its supporters everywhere challenged the determination of the question between Freedom and Slavery by a competition of emigration. Thus, while opening the Territory to Slavery, the bill also opened it to emigrants from every quarter, who might by their votes redress the wrong. The populous North, stung by a sharp sense of outrage, and inspired by a noble cause, poured into the debatable land, and promised soon to establish a supremacy of numbers there, involving, of course, a just supremacy of Freedom.

Then was conceived the consummation of the Crime against Kansas. What could not be accomplished peaceably, was to be accomplished forcibly. The reptile monster, that could not be quietly and securely hatched there, was to be pushed full-grown into the Territory. All efforts were now given to the dismal work of forcing Slavery on Free Soil. In flagrant derogation of the very Popular Sovereignty, whose name helped to impose this Bill upon the country, the atrocious object was now distinctly avowed. And the avowal has been followed by the act. Slavery has been forcibly introduced into Kansas, and placed under the formal safeguards of pretended law. How this was done, belongs to the argument.

In depicting this consummation, the simplest outline, without one word of color, will be best. Whether regarded in its mass or its details, in its origin or its result, it is all blackness, illumined by nothing from itself, but only by the heroism of the undaunted men and women, whom it environed. A plain statement of facts will be a picture of fearful truth, which faithful history will preserve in its darkest gallery. In the foreground all will recognise a familiar character, in himself a connecting link between the President and the border ruffian—less conspicuous for ability than for the exalted place he has occupied—who once sat in the seat where you now sit, sir; where once sat John Adams and Thomas Jefferson; also, where once sat Aaron Burr. I need not add the name of David R. Atchison. You have not forgotten that, at the session of Congress immediately succeeding the Nebraska Bill, he came tardily to his duty here, and then, after a short time, disappeared. The secret has been long since disclosed. Like Catiline, he stalked into this Chamber, reeking with conspiracy—*immo in Senatum venit*—and then like Catiline he skulked away—*abiit, excessit, evasit, erupit*—to join and provoke the conspirators, who at a distance awaited their congenial chief. Under the influence of his malign presence the Crime ripened to its fatal fruits, while the similitude with Catiline was again renewed in the sympathy, not even concealed, which he found in the very Senate itself, where, beyond even the Roman example, a Senator has not hesitated to appear as his open compurgator.

And now, as I proceed to show the way in which this Territory was overrun and finally subjugated to Slavery, I desire to remove in advance all question with regard to the authority on which I rely. The evidence is secondary; but it is the best which, in the nature of the case, can be had, and it is not less clear, direct, and peremptory, than any by which we are assured of the campaigns in the Crimea or the fall of Sevastopol. In its manifold mass, I confidently assert, that it is such a body of evidence as the human mind is not able to resist. It is found in the concurring reports of the public press; in the letters of correspondents; in the testimony of travellers; and in the unaffected story to which I have listened from leading citizens, who, during this winter, have "come flocking" here from that distant Territory. It breaks forth in the irrepressible outcry, reaching us from Kansas, in truthful tones, which leave no ground of mistake. It addresses us in formal complaints, instinct with the indignation of a people determined to be free, and unimpeachable as the declarations of a murdered man on his dying bed against his murderer. And let me add, that all this testimony finds an echo in the very statute-book of the conspirators, and also in language dropped from the President of the United States.

I begin with an admission from the President himself, in whose sight the people of Kansas have little favor. And yet, after arraigning the innocent emigrants from the North, he was constrained to declare that their conduct was "far from justifying the *illegal* and *reprehensible* counter-movement which ensued." Then, by the reluctant admission of the Chief Magistrate, there was a counter-movement, at once *illegal* and *reprehensible*. I thank thee, President, for teaching me these words; and I now put them in the front of this exposition, as in themselves a confession. Sir, this "illegal and reprehensible counter-movement" is none other than the dreadful Crime — under an apologetic *alias* — by which, through successive invasions, Slavery has been forcibly planted in this Territory.

Next to this Presidential admission must be placed the details of the invasions, which I now present as not only "illegal and reprehensible," but also unquestionable evidence of the resulting Crime.

The violence, for some time threatened, broke forth on the 29th November, 1854, at the first election of a Delegate to Congress, when companies from Missouri, amounting to upwards of one thousand, crossed into Kansas, and, with force and arms, proceeded to vote for Mr. Whitfield, the candidate of Slavery. An eye-witness, General Pomeroy, of superior intelligence and perfect integrity, thus describes this scene:

"The first ballot-box that was opened upon our virgin soil was closed to us by overpowering numbers and impending force. So bold and reckless were our invaders, that they cared not to conceal their attack. They came upon us not in the guise of voters, to steal away our franchise, but boldly and openly, to snatch it with a strong hand. They came directly from their own homes, and in compact and organized bands, with arms in hand and provisions for the expedition, marched to our polls, and, when their work was done, returned whence they came."

Here was an outrage at which the coolest blood of patriotism boils. Though, for various reasons unnecessary to develop, the busy settlers allowed the election to pass uncontested, still the means employed were none the less "illegal and reprehensible."

This infliction was a significant prelude to the grand invasion of the 30th March, 1855, at the election of the first Territorial Legislature under the organic law, when an armed multitude from Missouri entered the Territory, in larger numbers than General Taylor commanded at Buena Vista, or than General Jackson had within his lines at New Orleans—larger far than our fathers rallied on Bunker Hill. On they came as an "army with banners," organized in companies, with officers, munitions, tents, and provisions, as though marching upon a foreign foe, and breathing loud-mouthed threats that they would carry their purpose, if need be, by the bowie-knife and revolver. Among them, according to his own confession, was David R. Atchison, belted with the vulgar arms of his vulgar comrades. Arrived at their several destinations on the night before the election, the invaders pitched their tents, placed their sentries, and waited for the coming day. The same trustworthy eye-witness, whom I have already quoted, says, of one locality:

"Baggage-wagons were there with arms and ammunition enough for a protracted fight, and among them two brass field pieces, ready charged. They came with drums beating and flags flying and their leaders were of the most prominent and conspicuous men of their State."

Of another locality he says:

"The invaders came together in one armed and organized body, with trains of fifty wagons, besides horsemen, and, the night before election, pitched their camp in the vicinity of the polls; and, having appointed their own judges in place of those who, from intimidation or otherwise, failed to attend, they voted without any proof of residence."

With this force they were able, on the succeeding day, in some places, to intimidate the judges of elections; in others, to substitute judges of their own appointment; in others, to wrest the ballot-boxes from their rightful possessors, and everywhere to exercise a complete control of the election, and thus, by a preternatural audacity of usurpation, impose a Legislature upon the free people of Kansas. Thus was conquered the Sevastopol of that Territory!

But it was not enough to secure the Legislature. The election of a member of Congress recurred on the 2d October, 1855, and the same foreigners, who had learned their strength, again manifested it. Another invasion, in controlling numbers, came from Missouri, and once more forcibly exercised the electoral franchise in Kansas.

At last, in the latter days of November, 1855, a storm, long brewing, burst upon the heads of the devoted people. The ballot-boxes had been violated, and a Legislature installed, which had proceeded to carry out the conspiracy of the invaders; but the good people of the Territory, born to Freedom, and educated as American citizens, showed no signs of submission. Slavery, though recognised by pretended law, was in many places practically an outlaw. To the lawless borderers, this was hard to bear; and, like the Heathen of old, they raged, particularly against the town of Lawrence, already known, by the firmness of its principles and the character of its citizens, as the citadel of the good cause. On this account they threatened, in their peculiar language, to "wipe it out." Soon the hostile power was gathered for this purpose. The wickedness of this invasion was enhanced by the way in which it began. A citizen of Kansas, by the name of Dow, was murdered by one of the partisans of Slavery, under the name of "law and order." Such an outrage naturally aroused indignation and provoked threats. The professors of "law and order" allowed the murderer to escape; and, still further to illustrate the irony of the name they assumed, seized the friend of the murdered man, whose few neighbors soon rallied for his rescue. This transaction, though totally disregarded in its chief front of wickedness, became the excuse for unprecedented excitement. The weak Governor, with no faculty higher than servility to Slavery—whom the President, in his official delinquency, had appointed to a trust worthy only of a well-balanced character—was frightened from his propriety. By proclamation he invoked the Territory. By telegraph he invoked the President. The Territory would not respond to his senseless appeal. The President was dumb; but the proclamation was circulated throughout the border counties of Missouri; and Platte, Clay, Carlisle, Sabine, Howard, and Jefferson, each of them, contributed a volunteer company, recruited from the road sides, and armed with weapons which chance afforded—known as the "shot-gun militia"—with a Missouri officer as commissary general, dispensing rations, and another Missouri officer as general-in-chief; with two wagon loads of rifles, belonging to Missouri, drawn by six mules, from its arsenal at Jefferson City; with seven pieces of cannon, belonging to the United States, from its arsenal at Liberty; and this formidable force, amounting to at least 1,800 men, terrible with threats, with oaths, and with whisky, crossed the borders, and encamped in larger part at Wacherusa, over against the doomed town of Lawrence, which was now threatened with destruction. With these invaders was the Governor, who by this act levied war upon the people he was sent to protect. In camp with him was the original Catiline of the conspiracy, while by his side was the docile Chief Justice and the docile Judges. But this is not the first instance in which an unjust Governor has found tools where he ought to have found justice. In the great impeachment of Warren Hastings, the British orator, by whom it was conducted, exclaims, in words strictly applicable to the misdeed I now arraign, "Had he not the Chief Justice, the tamed and domesticated Chief Justice, who waited on him like a familiar spirit?" Thus was this invasion countenanced by those who should have stood in the breach against it. For more than a week it continued, while deadly conflict seemed imminent. I do not dwell on the heroism by which it was encountered, or the mean retreat to which it was compelled; for that is not necessary to exhibit the Crime which you are to judge. But I cannot forbear to add other additional features, furnished in the letter of a clergyman, written at the time, who saw and was a part of what he describes:

"Our citizens have been shot at, *and in two instances murdered*, our houses invaded, hay-ricks burnt, corn and other provisions plundered, cattle driven off, all communication cut off between us and the States, wagons on the way to us with provisions stopped and plundered, and the drivers taken prisoners, and we in hourly expectation of an attack. *Nearly every man has been in arms in the village.* Fortifications have been thrown up, by incessant labor night and day. The sound of the drum and the tramp of armed men resounded through our streets, *families fleeing with their household goods for safety.* Day before yesterday, the report of c[illegible]nnon was heard at our house, from the direction of Le[illegible]pton. Last Thursday, one of our neighbors—one of t[illegible]st peaceable and excellent of men, from Ohio—on [illegible] home, was set upon by a gang of twelve men on [illegible]k, and shot down. Over eight hundred men are g[illegible]der arms at Lawrence. As yet, no act of violence has been perpetrated by those on our side. *No blood of retaliation stains our hands. We stand and are ready to act purely in the defence of our homes and lives.*"

But the catalogue is not yet complete. On the 15th of December, when the people assembled to vote on the Constitution then submitted for adoption—only a few days after the Treaty of Peace between the Governor on the one side and the town of Lawrence on the other—another and fifth irruption was made. But I leave all this untold. Enough of these details has been given.

Five several times and more have these invaders entered Kansas in armed array, and thus five several times and more have they trampled upon the organic law of the Territory. But these extraordinary expeditions are simply the extraordinary witnesses to successive uninterrupted violence. They stand out conspicuous, but not alone. The spirit of evil, in which they had their origin, was wakeful and incessant. From the beginning, it hung upon the skirts of this interesting Territory, harrowing its peace, disturbing its prosperity, and keeping its inhabitants under the painful alarms of war. Thus was all Security of person, of property, and of labor, overthrown; and when I urge this incontrovertible fact, I set forth a wrong which is small only by the side of the giant wrong, for the consummation of which all this was done. Sir, what is man—what is government—without security; in the absence of which, nor man nor government can proceed in development or enjoy the fruits of existence? Without security, civilization is cramped and dwarfed. Without security, there can be no true Freedom. Nor shall I say too much, when I declare that security, guarded of course by its offspring, Freedom, is the true end and aim of government. Of this indispensable boon the people of Kansas have thus far been despoiled—absolutely, totally. All this is aggravated by the nature of their pursuits, rendering them peculiarly sensitive to interruption, and at the same time attesting their innocence. They are for the most part engaged in the cultivation of the soil, which from time immemorial has been the sweet employment of undisturbed industry. Contented in the returns of bounteous nature and the shade of his own trees, the husbandman is not aggressive; accustomed to produce, and not to destroy, he is essentially peaceful, unless his home is invaded, when his arm derives vigor from the soil he treads, and his soul inspiration from the heavens beneath whose canopy he daily toils. And such are the people of Kansas, whose Security has been overthrown. Scenes from which civilization averts her countenance have been a part of their daily life. The border incursions, which, in barbarous ages or barbarous lands, have fretted and "harried" an exposed people, have been here renewed, with this peculiarity, that our border robbers do not simply levy black mail and drive off a few cattle, like those who acted under the inspiration of the Douglas of other days; that they do not seize a few persons, and sweep them away into captivity, like the African slave-traders whom we brand as pirates; but that they commit a succession of acts, in which all border sorrows and all African wrongs are revived together on American soil, and which for the time being annuls all protection of all kinds, and enslaves the whole Territory.

Private griefs mingle their poignancy with public wrongs. I do not dwell on the anxieties which families have undergone, exposed to sudden assault, and obliged to lie down to rest with the alarms of war ringing in their ears, not knowing that another day might be spared to them. Throughout this bitter winter, with the thermometer at 30 degrees below zero, the citizens of Lawrence have been constrained to sleep under arms, with sentinels treading their constant watch against surprise. But our souls are wrung by individual instances. In vain do we condemn the cruelties of another age—the refinements of torture to which men have been doomed—the rack and thumb-screw of the Inquisition, the last agonies of the regicide Ravaillac—"Luke's iron crown; and Damien's bed of steel"—for kindred outrages have disgraced these borders. Murder has stalked—assassination has skulked in the tall grass of the prairie, and the vindictiveness of man has assumed unwonted forms. A preacher of the Gospel of the Saviour has been ridden on a rail, and then thrown into the Missouri, fastened to a log, and left to drift down its muddy, tortuous current. And lately we have had the tidings of that enormity without precedent—a deed without a name—where a candidate for the Legislature was most brutally gashed with knives and hatchets, and then, after weltering in blood on the snow-clad earth, was trundled along with gaping wounds, to fall dead in the face of his wife. It is common to drop a tear of sympathy over the trembling solicitudes of our early fathers, exposed to the stealthy assault of the savage foe; and an eminent American artist has pictured this scene in a marble group of rare beauty, on the front of the National Capitol, where the uplifted tomakawk is arrested by the strong arm and generous countenance of the pioneer, while his wife and children find shelter at his feet; but now the tear must be dropped over the trembling solicitudes of fellow-citizens, seeking to build a new State in Kansas, and exposed to the perpetual assault of murderous robbers from Missouri. Hirelings, picked from the drunken spew and vomit of an uneasy civilization—in the form of men—

> Aye, in the catalogue ye go for men;
> As hounds and gray hounds, mongrels, spaniels, curs,
> Shoughs, water-rugs, and demi-wolves, are called
> All by the name of dogs:

leashed together by secret signs and lodges, have renewed the incredible atrocities of the Assassins and of the Thugs; showing the blind submission of the Assassins to the Old Man of the Mountain, in robbing Christians on the road to Jerusalem, and showing the heartlessness of the Thugs, who, avowing that murder was their religion, waylaid travellers on the great road from Agra to Delhi; with the more deadly bowie-knife for the dagger of the Assassin, and the more deadly revolver for the noose of the Thug.

In these invasions, attended by the entire subversion of all Security in this Territory, with the plunder of the ballot-box, and the pollution of the electoral franchise, I show simply the process in unprecedented Crime. If that be the best Government, where an injury to a single citizen is resented as an injury to the whole State, then must our Government forfeit all claim to any such eminence, while it leaves its citizens thus exposed. In the outrage upon the ballot-box, even without the illicit fruits which I shall soon exhibit, there is a peculiar crime of the deepest dye, though subordinate to the final Crime, which should be promptly avenged. In countries where royalty is upheld, it is a special offence to rob the crown jewels, which are the emblems of that sovereignty before which the loyal subject bows, and it is treason to be found in adultery with the Queen, for in this way may a false heir be imposed upon the State; but in our Republic the ballot-box is the single priceless jewel of that sovereignty which we respect, and the electoral franchise, out of which are born the rulers of a free people, is the Queen whom we are to guard against pollution. In this plain presentment, whether as regards Security, or as regards Elections, there is enough, surely, without proceeding further, to justify the intervention of Congress, most promptly and completely, to throw over this oppressed people the impenetrable shield of the Constitution and laws. But the half is not yet told.

As every point in a wide-spread horizon radiates from a common centre, so everything said or done in this vast circle of Crime radiates from the *One Idea*, that Kansas, at all hazards, must be made a slave State. In all the manifold wickednesses that have occurred, and in every successive invasion, this *One Idea* has been ever present, as the Satanic tempter—the motive power—the *causing cause*.

To accomplish this result, three things were attempted: *first*, by outrages of all kinds to drive the friends of Freedom already there out of the Territory; *secondly*, to deter others from coming; and, *thirdly*, to obtain the complete control of the Government. The process of driving out, and also of deterring, has failed. On the contrary, the friends of Freedom there became more fixed in their resolves to stay and fight the battle, which they had never sought, but from which they disdained to retreat; while the friends of Freedom elsewhere were more aroused to the duty of timely succors, by men and munitions of just self-defence.

But, while defeated in the first two processes proposed, the conspirators succeeded in the last. By the violence already portrayed at the election of the 30th March, when the polls were occupied by the armed hordes from Missouri, they imposed a Legislature upon the Territory, and thus, under the iron mask of law, established a Usurpation not less complete than any in history. That this was done, I proceed to prove. Here is the evidence:

1. Only in this way can this extraordinary expedition be adequately explained. In the words of Moliere, once employed by John Quincy Adams in the other House, *Que diable allaient-ils faire dans cette galere?* What did they go into the Territory for? If their purposes were peaceful, as has been suggested, why cannons, arms, flags, numbers, and all this violence? As simple citizens, proceeding to the honest exercise of the electoral franchise, they might have gone with nothing more than a pilgrim's staff. Philosophy always seeks a *sufficient cause*, and only in the

One Idea, already presented, can a cause be found in any degree commensurate with this Crime; and this becomes so only when we consider the mad fanaticism of Slavery.

2. Public notoriety steps forward to confirm the suggestion of reason. In every place where Truth can freely travel, it has been asserted and understood, that the Legislature was imposed upon Kansas by foreigners from Missouri; and this universal voice is now received as undeniable verity.

3. It is also attested by the harangues of the conspirators. Here is what Stringfellow said *before* the invasion:

"To those who have qualms of conscience as to violating laws, State or National the time has come when such impositions must be disregarded, as your rights and property are in danger: *and I advise you, one and all, to enter every election district in Kansas, in defiance of Reeder and his vile myrmidons, and vote at the point of the bowie-knife and revolver.* Neither give nor take quarter, as our case demands it. It is enough that the slaveholding interest wills it, from which there is no appeal. What right has Governor Reeder to rule Missourians in Kansas? His proclamation and prescribed oath must be repudiated. It is your interest to do so. Mind that Slavery is established where it is not prohibited."

Here is what Atchison said *after* the invasion:

"Well what next? Why an election for members of the Legislature to organize the Territory must be held, What did I advise you to do then? Why, meet them on their own ground, and beat them at their own game again; and cold and inclement as the weather was, I went over with a company of men. My object in going was not to vote. I had no right to vote, unless I had disfranchised myself in Missouri. I was not within two miles of a voting place. My object in going was not to vote, but to settle a difficulty between two of our candidates: and the Abolitionists of the North said, *and published it abroad, that Atchison was there with bowie-knife and revolver, and by God 'twas true. I never did go into that Territory—I never intend to go into that Territory—without being prepared for all such kind of cattle.* Well, we beat them, and Governor Reeder gave certificates to a majority of all the members of both Houses, and then, after they were organized, as everybody will admit, they were the only competent persons to say who were, and who were not, members of the same."

4. It is confirmed by the contemporaneous admission of the *Squatter Sovereign*, a paper published at Atchison, and at once the organ of the President and of these Borderers, which, under date of 1st April, thus recounts the victory:

"INDEPENDENCE, [MISSOURI,] *March* 31, 1855.

"Several hundred emigrants from Kansas have just entered our city. They were preceded by the Westport and Independence brass bands. They came in at the west side of the public square, and proceeded entirely around it, the bands cheering us with fine music, and the emigrants with good news. Immediately following the bands were about two hundred horsemen in regular order; following these were one hundred and fifty wagons, carriages, &c. They gave repeated cheers for Kansas and Missouri. They report that not an Anti-Slavery man will be in the Legislature of Kansas. *We have made a clean sweep.*"

5. It is also confirmed by the contemporaneous testimony of another paper, always faithful to Slavery, the New York *Herald*, in the letter of a correspondent from Brunswick, in Missouri, under date of 20th April, 1855:

"From five to seven thousand men started from Missouri to attend the election, some to remove, but the most to return to their families, with an intention, if they liked the Territory, to make it their permanent abode at the earliest moment practicable. But they intended to vote. The Missourians were, many of them, Douglas men. There were one hundred and fifty voters from this county, one hundred and seventy-five from Howard, one hundred from Cooper. Indeed every county furnished its quota; and when they set out, it looked like an army." * * * "They were armed." * * * * "And, as there were no houses in the Territory, they carried tents. Their mission was a peaceable one—to vote, and to drive down stakes for their future homes. After the election, some one thousand five hundred of the voters sent a committee to Mr. Reeder, to ascertain if it was his purpose to ratify the election. He answered that it was, and said the majority at an election must carry the day. But it is not to be denied that the one thousand five hundred, apprehending that the Governor might attempt to play the tyrant—since his conduct had already been insidious and unjust—wore on their hats bunches of hemp. They were resolved, if a tyrant attempted to trample upon the rights of the sovereign people, to hang him."

6. It is again confirmed by the testimony of a lady, who for five years has lived in Western Missouri, and thus writes in a letter published in the *New Haven Register*:

"MIAMI, SALINE CO., *November* 26, 1855.

"You ask me to tell you something about the Kansas and Missouri troubles. Of course you know in what they have originated. *There is no denying that the Missourians have determined to control the elections, if possible;* and I don't know that their measures would be justifiable, except upon the principle of self-preservation; and that, you know, is the first law of nature."

7. And it is confirmed still further by the Circular of the Emigration Society of Lafayette, in Missouri, dated as late as 25th March, 1856, in which the efforts of Missourians are openly confessed:

"The Western counties of Missouri have for the last two years been heavily taxed, both in money and time, in fighting the battles of the South. *Lafayette county alone has expended more than $100,000 in money, and as much or more in time. Up to this time, the border counties of Missouri have upheld and maintained the rights and interests of the South in this struggle, unassisted, and not unsuccessfully.* But the Abolitionists, staking their all upon the Kansas issue, and hesitating at no means, fair or foul, are moving heaven and earth to render that beautiful Territory a *Free State.*"

8. Here, also, is complete admission of the Usurpation, by the *Intelligencer*, a leading paper of St. Louis, Missouri, made in the ensuing summer:

"Atchison and Stringfellow, with their Missouri followers, overwhelmed the settlers in Kansas, browbeat and bullied them, and took the Government from their hands. Missouri votes elected the present body of men who insult public intelligence and popular rights by styling themselves 'the Legislature of Kansas.' This body of men are helping themselves to fat speculations by locating the 'seat of Government' and getting town lots for their votes. They are passing laws disfranchising all the citizens of Kansas who do not believe Negro Slavery to be a Christian institution and a national blessing. They are proposing to punish with imprisonment the utterance of views inconsistent with their own. And they are trying to perpetuate their preposterous and infernal tyranny by appointing *for a term of years* creatures of their own, as commissioners in every county, to lay and collect taxes, and see that the laws they are passing are faithfully executed. Has this age anything to compare with these acts in audacity?"

9. In harmony with all these is the authoritative declaration of Governor Reeder, in a speech addressed to his neighbors, at Easton, Pennsylvania, at the end of April, 1855, and immediately afterwards published in the Washington *Union*. Here it is:

"It was indeed too true that Kansas had been invaded, conquered, subjugated, by an armed force from beyond her borders, led on by a fanatical spirit, trampling under foot the principles of the Kansas bill and the right of suffrage."

10. And in similar harmony is the complaint of the people of Kansas, in a public meeting at Big Springs, on the 5th September, 1855, embodied in these words:

> "*Resolved*, That the body of men who for the last two months have been passing laws for the people of our Territory, moved, counselled, and dictated to by the demagogues of Missouri, are to us a foreign body, representing only the lawless invaders who elected them, and not the people of the Territory—that we repudiate their action, as the monstrous consummation of an act of violence, usurpation, and fraud, unparalleled in the history of the Union, and worthy only of men unfitted for the duties and regardless of the responsibilities of Republicans."

11. And finally, by the official minutes, which have been laid on our table by the President, the invasion, which ended in the Usurpation, is clearly established; but the effect of this testimony has been so amply exposed by the Senator from Vermont, [Mr. COLLAMER,] in his able and indefatigable argument, that I content myself with simply referring to it.

On this cumulative, irresistible evidence, in concurrence with the antecedent history, I rest. And yet Senators here have argued that this cannot be so—precisely as the conspiracy of Catiline was doubted in the Roman Senate. *Nonnulli sunt in hoc ordine, qui aut ea, quæ imminent, non videant; aut ea, quæ vident, dissimulent; qui spem Catilinæ mollibus sententiis aluerunt, conjurationemque nascentem non credendo corroboraverunt.* As I listened to the Senator from Illinois, while he painfully strove to show that there was no Usurpation, I was reminded of the effort by a distinguished logician, in a much-admired argument, to prove that Napoleon Bonaparte never existed. And permit me to say, that the fact of his existence is not placed more completely above doubt than the fact of this Usurpation. This I assert on the proofs already presented. But confirmation comes almost while I speak. The columns of the public press are now daily filled with testimony, solemnly taken before the Committee of Congress in Kansas, which shows, in awful light, the violence ending in the Usurpation. Of this I may speak on some other occasion. Meanwhile, I proceed with the development of the Crime.

The usurping Legislature assembled at the appointed place in the interior, and then at once, in opposition to the veto of the Governor, by a majority of two-thirds, removed to the Shawnee Mission, a place in most convenient proximity to the Missouri borderers, by whom it had been constituted, and whose tyrannical agent it was. The statutes of Missouri, in all their text, with their divisions and subdivisions, were adopted bodily, and with such little local adaptation that the word "State" in the original is not even changed to "Territory," but is left to be corrected by an explanatory act. But, all this general legislation was entirely subordinate to the special act, entitled "An Act to punish offences against Slave Property," in which the One Idea, that provoked this whole conspiracy, is at last embodied in legislative form, and Human Slavery openly recognised on Free Soil, under the sanction of pretended law. This act of thirteen sections is in itself a *Dance of Death.* But its complex completeness of wickedness, without a parallel, may be partially conceived, when it is understood that in three sections only of it is the penalty of death denounced no less than forty-eight different times, by as many changes of language, against the heinous offence, described in forty-eight different ways, of interfering with what does not exist in that Territory—and under the Constitution cannot exist there—I mean property in human flesh. Thus is Liberty sacrificed to Slavery, and Death summoned to sit at the gates as guardian of the Wrong.

But the work of Usurpation was not perfected even yet. It had already cost too much to be left at any hazard.

> ——————"To be thus was nothing;
> But to be safely thus!"

Such was the object. And this could not be, except by the entire prostration of all the safeguards of Human Rights. The liberty of speech, which is the very breath of a Republic; the press, which is the terror of wrong-doers; the bar, through which the oppressed beards the arrogance of law; the jury, by which right is vindicated; all these must be struck down, while officers are provided, in all places, ready to be the tools of this tyranny; and then, to obtain final assurance that their crime was secure, the whole Usurpation, stretching over the Territory, must be fastened and riveted by legislative bolts, spikes, and screws, *so as to defy all effort at change through the ordinary forms of law.* To this work, in its various parts, were bent the subtlest energies; and never, from Tubal Cain to this hour, was any fabric forged with more desperate skill and completeness.

Mark, sir, three different legislative enactments, which constitute part of this work. *First*, according to one act, all who deny, by spoken or written word, "the right of persons to hold slaves in this Territory," are denounced as felons, to be punished by imprisonment at hard labor, for a term not less than two years; it may be for life. And to show the extravagance of this injustice, it has been well put by the Senator from Vermont, [Mr. COLLAMER,] that should the Senator from Michigan, [Mr. CASS,] who believes that Slavery cannot exist in a Territory, unless introduced by express legislative acts, venture there with his moderate opinions, his doom must be that of a felon! To this extent are the great liberties of speech and of the press subverted. *Secondly*, by another act, entitled "An Act concerning Attorneys-at-Law," no person can practice as an attorney, unless he *shall obtain a license* from the Territorial courts, which, of course, a tyrannical discretion will be free to deny; and after obtaining such license, he is constrained to take an oath, not only "to support" the Constitution of the United States, but also "to support and sustain"—mark here the reduplication—the Territorial act, and the Fugitive Slave Bill, thus erecting a test for the function of the bar, calculated to exclude citizens who honestly regard that latter legislative enormity as unfit to be obeyed. And, *thirdly*, by another act, entitled "An Act concerning Jurors," all persons "conscientiously opposed to holding slaves," or "not admitting the right to hold slaves in the Territory," are excluded from the jury on every question, civil or criminal, arising out of asserted slave property; while, in all cases, the summoning of the jury is left without one word of restraint to "the marshal, sheriff, or other officer," who are thus free to pack it according to their tyrannical discretion.

For the ready enforcement of all statutes against Human Freedom, the President had already furnished a powerful quota of officers, in the Governor, Chief Justice, Judges, Secretary, Attorney, and Marshal. The Legislature completed this part of the work, by constituting, in each county, a *Board of Commissioners*, composed of two persons, associated with the Probate Judge, whose duty it is "to appoint a county treasurer, coroner, justices of the peace, constables, and *all* other officers provided for by law," and then proceeded to the choice of this very Board; thus delegating and diffusing their usurped power, and tyrannically imposing upon the Territory a crowd of officers, in whose appointment the people have had no voice, directly or indirectly.

And still the final inexorable work remained. A Legislature, renovated in both branches, could not assemble until 1858, so that, during this long intermediate period, this whole system must continue in the likeness of law, unless overturned by the Federal Government, or, in default of such interposition, by a generous uprising of an oppressed people. But it was necessary to guard against the possibility of change, even tardily, at a future election; and this was done by two different acts; under the *first* of which, all who will not take the oath to support the Fugitive Slave Bill are excluded from the elective franchise; and under the *second* of which, all others are entitled to vote who shall tender a tax of one dollar to the Sheriff on the day of election; thus, by provision of Territorial law, disfranchising all opposed to Slavery, and at the same time opening the door to the votes of the invaders; by an unconstitutional shibboleth, excluding from the polls the mass of actual settlers, and by making the franchise depend upon a petty tax only, admitting to the polls the mass of borderers from Missouri. Thus, by tyrannical forethought, the Usurpation not only fortified all that it did, but assumed a *self-perpetuating* energy.

Thus was the Crime consummated. Slavery now stands erect, clanking its chains on the Territory of Kansas, surrounded by a code of death, and trampling upon all cherished liberties, whether of speech, the press, the bar, the trial by jury, or the electoral franchise. And, sir, all this has been done, not merely to introduce a wrong which in itself is a denial of all rights, and in dread of which a mother has lately taken the life of her offspring; not merely, as has been sometimes said, to protect Slavery in Missouri, since it is futile for this State to complain of Freedom on the side of Kansas, when Freedom exists without complaint on the side of Iowa and also on the side of Illinois; but it has been done for the sake of political power, in order to bring two new slaveholding Senators upon this floor, and thus to fortify in the National Government the desperate chances of a waning Oligarchy. As the ship, voyaging on pleasant summer seas, is assailed by a pirate crew, and robbed for the sake of its doubloons and dollars—so is this beautiful Territory now assailed in its peace and prosperity, and robbed, in order to wrest its political power to the side of Slavery. Even now the black flag of the land pirates from Missouri waves at the mast head; in their laws you hear the pirate yell, and see the flash of the pirate knife; while, incredible to relate! the President, gathering the Slave Power at his back, testifies a pirate sympathy.

Sir, all this was done in the name of Popular Sovereignty. And this is the close of the tragedy. Popular Sovereignty, which, when truly understood, is a fountain of just power, has ended in Popular Slavery; not merely in the subjection of the unhappy African race, but of this proud Caucasian blood, which you boast. The profession with which you began, of *All by the People*, has been lost in the wretched reality of *Nothing for the People*. Popular Sovereignty, in whose deceitful name plighted faith was broken, and an ancient Landmark of Freedom was overturned, now lifts itself before us, like Sin, in the terrible picture of Milton,

> "That seemed a woman to the waist, and fair,
> But ended foul in many a scaly fold
> Voluminous and vast, a serpent armed
> With mortal sting; about her middle round
> A cry of hell-hounds never ceasing barked
> With wide Cerberean mouths full loud, and rung
> A hideous peal; yet, when they list, would creep,
> If aught disturbed their noise, into her womb,
> And kennel there, yet there still barked and howled
> Within, unseen."

The image is complete at all points; and, with this exposure, I take my leave of the Crime against Kansas.

II. Emerging from all the blackness of this Crime, in which we seem to have been lost, as in a savage wood, and turning our backs upon it, as upon desolation and death, from which, while others have suffered, we have escaped, I come now to THE APOLOGIES which the Crime has found. Sir, well may you start at the suggestion that such a series of wrongs, so clearly proved by various testimony, so openly confessed by the wrong-doers, and so widely recognised throughout the country, should find Apologies. But the partisan spirit, now, as in other days, hesitates at nothing. The great Crimes of history have never been without Apologies. The massacre of St. Bartholomew, which you now instinctively condemn, was, at the time, applauded in high quarters, and even commemorated by a Papal medal, which may still be procured at Rome; as the Crime against Kansas, which is hardly less conspicuous in dreadful eminence, has been shielded on this floor by extenuating words, and even by a Presidential message, which, like the Papal medal, can never be forgotten in considering the madness and perversity of men.

Sir, the Crime cannot be denied. The President himself has admitted "illegal and reprehensible" conduct. To such conclusion he was compelled by irresistible evidence; but what he mildly describes I openly arraign. Senators may affect to put it aside by a sneer; or to reason it away by figures; or to explain it by a theory, such as desperate invention has produced on this floor, that the Assassins and Thugs of Missouri were in reality citizens of Kansas; but all these efforts, so far as made, are only tokens of the weakness of the cause, while to the original Crime they add another offence of false testimony against innocent and suffering men. But the Apologies for the Crime are worse than the efforts at denial. In cruelty and heartlessness they identify their authors with the great trangression.

They are four in number, and four-fold in character. The first is the Apology *tyrannical;* the second, the Apology *imbecile;* the third, the Apology *absurd;* and the fourth, the Apology *infamous*. This is all. Tyranny, imbecility, absurdity, and infamy, all unite to dance, like the weird sisters, about this Crime.

The Apology *tyrannical* is founded on the mistaken act of Governor Reeder, in authenticating the Usurping Legislature, by which it is asserted that, whatever may have been the actual force or fraud in its election, the people of Kansas are effectually concluded, and the whole proceeding is placed under the formal sanction of law. According to this assumption, complaint is now in vain, and it only remains that Congress should sit and hearken to it, without correcting the wrong, as the ancient tyrant listened and granted no redress to the human moans that issued from the heated brazen bull, which subtle cruelty had devised. This I call the Apology of technicality inspired by tyranny.

The facts on this head are few and plain. Governor Reeder, after allowing only five days for objections to the returns—a space of time unreasonably brief in that extensive Territory—declared a majority of the members of the Council and of the House of Representatives "duly elected," withheld certificates from certain others, because of satisfactory proof that they were not duly elected, and appointed a day for new elections to supply these vacancies. Afterwards, by formal message, he recognised the Legislature as a legal body, and when he vetoed their act of adjournment to the neighborhood of Missouri, he did it simply on the ground of the illegality of such an adjournment under the organic law. Now, to every assumption founded on these facts, there are two satisfactory replies; *first*, that no certificate of the Governor can do more than authenticate a subsisting legal act, without of itself infusing legality where the essence of legality is not already; and *secondly*, that violence or fraud, wherever disclosed, vitiates completely every proceeding. In denying these principles, you place the certificate above the thing certified, and give a perpetual lease to violence and fraud, merely because at an ephemeral moment they were unquestioned. This will not do.

Sir, I am no apologist for Governor Reeder. There is sad reason to believe that he went to Kansas originally as the tool of the President; but his simple nature, nurtured in the atmosphere of Pennsylvania, revolted at the service required, and he turned from his patron to duty. Grievously did he err in yielding to the Legislature any act of authentication; but he has in some measure answered for this error by determined efforts since to expose the utter illegality of that body, which he now repudiates entirely. It was said of certain Roman Emperors, who did infinite mischief in their beginnings, and infinite good towards their ends, that they should never have been born, or never died; and I would apply the same to the official life of this Kansas Governor. At all events, I dismiss the Apology founded on his acts, as the utterance of tyranny by the voice of law, transcending the declaration of the pedantic judge, in the British Parliament, on the eve of our Revolution, that our fathers, notwithstanding their complaints, were in reality represented in Parliament, inasmuch as their lands, under the original charters, were held "in common socage, as of the manor of Greenwich in Kent," which, being duly represented, carried with it all the Colonies. Thus in other ages has tyranny assumed the voice of law.

Next comes the Apology *imbecile*, which is founded on the alleged want of power in the President to arrest this Crime. It is openly asserted, that, under the existing laws of the United States, the Chief Magistrate had no authority to interfere in Kansas for this purpose. Such is the broad statement, which, even if correct, furnishes no Apology for any proposed ratification of the Crime, but which is in reality untrue; and this, I call the Apology of imbecility.

In other matters, no such ostentatious imbecility appears. Only lately, a vessel of war in the Pacific has chastised the cannibals of the Fejee Islands, for alleged outrages on American citizens. But no person of ordinary intelligence will pretend that American citizens in the Pacific have received wrongs from these cannibals comparable in atrocity to those received by American citizens in Kansas. Ah, sir, the interests of Slavery are not touched by any chastisement of the Fejees!

Constantly we are informed of efforts at New York, through the agency of the Government, and sometimes only on the breath of suspicion, to arrest vessels about to sail on foreign voyages in violation of our neutrality laws or treaty stipulations. Now, no man familiar with the cases will presume to suggest that the urgency for these arrests was equal to the urgency for interposition against these successive invasions from Missouri. But the Slave Power is not disturbed by such arrests at New York!

At this moment, the President exults in the vigilance with which he has prevented the enlistment of a few soldiers, to be carried off to Halifax, in violation of our territorial sovereignty, and England is bravely threatened, even to the extent of a rupture of diplomatic relations, for her endeavor, though unsuccessful, and at once abandoned. Surely, no man in his senses will urge that this act was anything but trivial by the side of the Crime against Kansas. But the Slave Power is not concerned in this controversy.

Thus, where the Slave Power is indifferent, the President will see that the laws are faithfully executed; but, in other cases, where the interests of Slavery are at stake, he is controlled absolutely by this tyranny, ready at all times to do, or not to do, precisely as it dictates. Therefore it is, that Kansas is left a prey to the Propagandists of Slavery, while the whole Treasury, the Army and Navy of the United States, are lavished to hunt a single slave through the streets of Boston. You have not forgotten the latter instance; but I choose to refresh it in your minds.

As long ago as 1851, the War Department and Navy Department concurred in placing the forces of the United States, near Boston, at the command of the Marshal, if needed, for the enforcement of an Act of Congress, which had no support in the public conscience, as I believe it has no support in the Constitution; and thus these forces were degraded to the loathsome work of slave-hunters. More than three years afterwards, an occasion arose for their intervention. A fugitive from Virginia, who for some days had trod the streets of Boston as a freeman, was seized as a slave. The whole community was aroused, while Bunker Hill and Faneuil Hall quaked with responsive indignation. Then, sir, the President, anxious that no tittle of Slavery should suffer, was curiously eager in the enforcement of the statute. The despatches between him and his agents in Boston attest his zeal. Here are some of them:

BOSTON, *May* 27, 1854.

To the President of the United States:

In consequence of an attack upon the Court-house last night, for the purpose of rescuing a fugitive slave under arrest, and in which one of my own guards was killed, *I have availed myself of the resources of the United States, placed under my control by letter from the War and Navy Departments, in* 1851, and now have two companies of Troops, from Fort Independence, stationed in the Court-house. Everything is now quiet. The attack was repulsed by my own guard.

WATSON FREEMAN.
United States Marshal, Boston, Mass.

WASHINGTON, *May* 27, 1854.

To Watson Freeman.
United States Marshal, Boston, Mass.:

Your conduct is approved. The law must be executed.

FRANKLIN PIERCE.

WASHINGTON, *May* 30, 1854.

To Hon. B. F. Hallett, Boston, Mass.:

What is the state of the case of Burns?

SIDNEY WEBSTER.
[*Private Secretary of the President.*]

WASHINGTON, *May* 31, 1854.

To B. F. Hallett,
United States Attorney, Boston, Mass.:

Incur any expense deemed necessary by the Marshal and yourself, for City Military, or otherwise, to insure the execution of the law.

FRANKLIN PIERCE.

But the President was not content with such forces as were then on hand in the neighborhood. Other posts also were put under requisition. Two companies of National troops, stationed at New York, were kept under arms, ready at any moment to proceed to Boston; and the Adjutant General of the Army was directed to repair to the scene, there to superintend the execution of the statute. All this was done for the sake of Slavery; but during long months of menace suspended over the Free Soil of Kansas, breaking forth in successive invasions, the President has folded his hands in complete listlessness, or, if he has moved at all, it has been only to encourage the robber Propagandists.

And now the intelligence of the country is insulted by the Apology, that the President had no power to interfere. Why, sir, to make this confession is to confess our Government to be a practical failure—which I will never do, except, indeed, as it is administered now. No, sir; the imbecility of the Chief Magistrate shall not be charged upon our American Institutions. Where there is a will, there is a way; and in his case, had the will existed, there would have been a way, easy and triumphant, to guard against the Crime we now deplore. His powers were in every respect ample; and this I will prove by the statute book. By the Act of Congress of 28th February, 1795, it is enacted, "that whenever the laws of the United States shall be opposed, *or the execution thereof obstructed*, in any State, by combinations too powerful to be suppressed by the ordinary course of judicial proceedings, or by the powers vested in the marshals," the President "may call forth the militia." By the supplementary Act of 3d March, 1807, in all cases where he is authorized to call forth the militia "for the purpose of causing the laws to be duly executed," the President is further empowered, in any State *or Territory*, "to employ for the same purposes such part of the land or naval force of the United States as shall be judged necessary." There is the letter of the law; and you will please to mark the power conferred. In no case where the *laws of the United States* are *opposed*, or their execution *obstructed*, is the President constrained to wait for the requisition of a Governor, or even the petition of a citizen. Just so soon as he learns the fact, no matter by what channel, he is invested by law with full power to counteract it. True it is, that when the *laws of a State* are obstructed, he can interfere only on the application of the Legislature of such State, or of the Executive, when the Legislature cannot be convened; but when the Federal laws are obstructed, no such preliminary application is necessary. It is his high duty, under his oath of office, to see that they are executed, and, if need be, by the Federal forces.

And, sir, this is the precise exigency that has arisen in Kansas—precisely this; nor more, nor less. The Act of Congress, constituting the very *organic law* of the Territory, which, in peculiar phrase, as if to avoid ambiguity, declares, as "its true intent and meaning," that the people thereof "shall be left perfectly free to form and regulate their domestic institutions in their own way," has been from the beginning *opposed* and *obstructed* in its execution. If the President had power to employ the Federal forces in Boston, when he supposed the Fugitive Slave Bill was obstructed, and merely in anticipation of such obstruction, it is absurd to say that he had not power in Kansas, when, in the face of the whole country, the very *organic law* of the Territory was trampled under foot by successive invasions, and the freedom of the people there overthrown. To assert ignorance of this obstruction—premeditated, long-continued, and stretching through months—attributes to him not merely imbecility, but idiocy. And thus do I dispose of this Apology.

Next comes the Apology *absurd*, which is, indeed, in the nature of a pretext. It is alleged that a small printed pamphlet, containing the "Constitution and Ritual of the Grand Encampment and Regiments of the Kansas Legion," was taken from the person of one George F. Warren, who attempted to avoid detection by chewing it. The oaths and grandiose titles of the pretended Legion have all been set forth, and this poor mummery of a secret society, which existed only on paper, has been gravely introduced on this floor, in order to extenuate the Crime against Kansas. It has been paraded in more than one speech, and even stuffed into the report of the committee.

A part of the obligations assumed by the members of this Legion shows why it has been thus pursued, and also attests its innocence. It is as follows:

"I will never knowingly propose a person for membership in this order *who is not in favor of making Kansas a free State*, and whom I feel satisfied will exert his entire influence to bring about this result. I will support, maintain, and abide by any honorable movement made by the organization to secure this great end, *which will not conflict with the laws of the country and the Constitution of the United States*."

Kansas is to be made a free State, by an honorable movement, which will not conflict with the laws and the Constitution. That is the object of the organization, declared in the very words of the initiatory obligation. Where is the wrong in this? What is there here, which can cast reproach, or even suspicion, upon the people of Kansas? Grant that the Legion was constituted, can you extract from it any Apology for the original Crime, or for its present ratification? Secret societies, with their extravagant oaths, are justly offensive; but who can find, in this mistaken machinery, any excuse for the denial of all rights to the people of Kansas? All this, I say, on the supposition that the society was a reality, which it was not. Existing in the fantastic brains of a few persons only, it never had any practical life. It was never organized. The whole tale, with the mode of obtaining the copy of the Constitution, is at once a cock-and-bull story and a mare's nest; trivial as the former; absurd as the latter; and to be dismissed, with the Apology founded upon it, to the derision which triviality and absurdity justly receive.

It only remains, under this head, that I should speak of the Apology *infamous;* founded on false testimony against the Emigrant Aid Company, and assumptions of duty more false than the testimony. Defying Truth and mocking Decency, this Apology excels all others in futility and audacity, while, from its utter hollowness, it proves the utter impotence of the conspirators to defend their Crime. Falsehood, always *infamous*, in this case arouses peculiar scorn. An association of sincere benevolence, faithful to the Constitution and laws, whose only fortifications are hotels, school-houses, and churches; whose only weapons are saw-mills, tools, and books; whose mission is peace and good will, has been falsely assailed on this floor, and an errand of blameless virtue has been made the pretext for an unpardonable Crime. Nay, more—the innocent are sacrificed, and the guilty set at liberty. They who seek to do the mission of the Saviour are scourged and crucified, while the murderer, Barabbas, with the sympathy of the chief priests, goes at large.

Were I to take counsel of my own feelings, I should dismiss this whole Apology to the ineffable contempt which it deserves; but it has been made to play such a part in this conspiracy, that I feel it a duty to expose it completely.

Sir, from the earliest times, men have recognised the advantages of organization, as an effective agency in promoting works of peace or war. Especially at this moment, there is no interest, public or private, high or low, of charity or trade, of luxury or convenience, which does not seek its aid. Men organize to rear churches and to sell thread; to build schools and to sail ships; to construct roads and to manufacture toys; to spin cotton and to print books; to weave cloths and to quicken harvests; to provide food and to distribute light; to influence Public Opinion and to secure votes; to guard infancy in its weakness, old age in its decrepitude, and womanhood in its wretchedness; and now, in all large towns, when death has come, they are buried by organized societies, and, emigrants to another world, they lie down in pleasant places, adorned by organized skill. To complain that this prevailing principle has been applied to living emigration is to complain of Providence and the irresistible tendencies implanted in man.

But this application of the principle is no recent invention, brought forth for an existing emergency. It has the best stamp of Antiquity. It showed itself in the brightest days of Greece, where colonists moved in organized bands. It became a part of the mature policy of Rome, where bodies of men were constituted expressly for this purpose, *triumviri ad colonos deducendos*.—(Livy, xxxvii, § 46.) Naturally it has been accepted in modern times by every civilized State. With the sanction of Spain, an association of Genoese merchants first introduced slaves to this continent. With the sanction of France, the Society of Jesuits stretched their labors over Canada and the Great Lakes to the Mississippi. It was under the auspices of Emigrant Aid Companies, that our country was originally settled, by the Pilgrim Fathers of Plymouth, by the adventurers of Virginia, and by the philanthropic Oglethorpe, whose "benevolence of soul," commemorated by Pope, sought to plant a Free State in Georgia. At this day, such associations, of a humbler character, are found in Europe, with offices in the great capitals, through whose activity emigrants are directed here.

For a long time, emigration to the West, from the Northern and Middle States, but particularly from New England, has been of marked significance. In quest of better homes, annually it has pressed to the unsettled lands, in numbers to be counted by tens of thousands; but this has been done heretofore with little knowledge, and without guide or counsel. Finally, when, by the establishment of a Government in Kansas, the tempting fields of that central region were opened to the competition of peaceful colonization, and especially when it was declared that the question of Freedom or Slavery there was to be determined by the votes of actual settlers, then at once was organization enlisted as an effective agency in quickening and conducting the emigration impelled thither, and, more than all, in providing homes for it on arrival there.

The Company was first constituted under an act of the Legislature of Massachusetts, 4th of May, 1854, some weeks prior to the passage of the Nebraska bill. The original act of incorporation was subsequently abandoned, and a new charter received in February, 1855, in which the objects of the Society are thus declared:

"For the purposes of directing emigration Westward. and *aiding in providing accommodations for the emigrants after arriving at their places of destination.*"

At any other moment, an association for these purposes would have taken its place, by general consent, among the philanthropic experiments of the age; but Crime is always suspicious, and shakes, like a sick man, merely at the pointing of a finger. The conspirators against Freedom in Kansas now shook with tremor, real or affected. Their wicked plot was about to fail. To help themselves, they denounced the Emigrant Aid Company; and their denunciations, after finding an echo in the President, have been repeated, with much particularity, on this floor, in the formal report of your committee.

The falsehood of the whole accusation will appear in illustrative specimens.

A charter is set out, section by section, which, though originally granted, was subsequently abandoned, and is not in reality the charter of the Company, but is materially unlike it.

The Company is represented as "a powerful corporation, with a capital of five millions;" when, by its actual charter, it is not allowed to hold property above one million, and, in point of fact, its capital has not exceeded $100,000.

Then, again, it is suggested, if not alleged, that this enormous capital, which I have already said does not exist, is invested in "cannon and rifles, in powder and lead, and implements of war"—all of which, whether alleged or suggested, is absolutely false. The officers of the Company authorize me to give to this whole pretension a point-blank denial.

All these allegations are of small importance, and I mention them only because they show the character of the report, and also something of the quicksand on which the Senator from Illinois has chosen to plant himself. But these are all capped by the unblushing assertion that the proceedings of the Company were "in perversion of the plain provisions of an Act of Congress;" and also, another unblushing assertion, as "certain and undeniable," that the Company was formed to promote certain objects, "regardless of the rights and wishes of the people, as guarantied by the Constitution of the United States, and secured by their organic law;" when it is certain and undeniable that the Company has done nothing in perversion of any Act of Congress, while to the extent of its power it has sought to protect the rights and wishes of the actual people in the Territory.

Sir, this Company has violated in no respect the Constitution or laws of the land; not in the severest letter or the slightest spirit. But every other imputation is equally baseless. It is not true, as the Senator from Illinois has alleged, in order in some way to compromise the Company, that it was informed before the public of the date fixed for the election of the Legislature. This statement is pronounced by the Secretary, in a letter now before me, "an unqualified falsehood, not having even the shadow of a shade of truth for its basis." It is not true that men have been hired by the Company to go to Kansas; for every emigrant, who has gone under its direction, has himself provided the means for his journey. Of course, sir, it is not true, as has been complained by the Senator from South Carolina, with that proclivity to error which marks all his utterances, that men have been sent by the Company "with one uniform gun, Sharpe's rifle;" for it has supplied no arms of any kind to anybody. It is not true that the Company has encouraged any fanatical aggression upon the people of Missouri; for it has counselled order, peace, forbearance. It is not true that the Company has chosen its emigrants on account of their political opinions; for it has asked no questions with regard to the opinions of any whom it aids, and at this moment stands ready to forward those from the South as well as the North, while, in the Territory, all, from whatever quarter, are admitted to an equal enjoyment of its tempting advantages. It is not true that the Company has sent persons merely to control elections, and not to remain in the Territory; for its whole action, and all its anticipation of pecuniary profits, are founded on the hope to stock the country with permanent settlers, by whose labor the capital of the Company shall be made to yield its increase, and by whose fixed interest in the soil the welfare of all shall be promoted.

Sir, it has not the honor of being an Abolition Society, or of numbering among its officers Abolitionists. Its President is a retired citizen, of ample means and charitable life, who has taken no part in the conflicts on Slavery, and has never allowed his sympathies to be felt by Abolitionists. One of its Vice Presidents is a gentleman from Virginia, with family and friends there, who has always opposed the Abolitionists. Its generous Treasurer, who is now justly absorbed by the objects of the Company, has always been understood as ranging with his extensive connexions, by blood and marriage, on the side of that quietism which submits to all the tyranny of the Slave Power. Its Directors are more conspicuous for wealth and science, than for any activity against Slavery. Among these is an eminent lawyer of Massachusetts, Mr. Chapman—personally known, doubtless, to some who hear me—who has distinguished himself by an austere conservatism, too natural to the atmosphere of courts, which does not flinch even from the support of the Fugitive Slave Bill. In a recent address at a public meeting in Springfield, this gentleman thus speaks for himself and his associates:

"I have been a Director of the Society from the first, and have kept myself well informed in regard to its proceedings. I am not aware that any one in this community ever suspected me of being an Abolitionist: but I have been accused of being Pro-Slavery; and I believe many good people think I am quite too conservative on that subject. I take this occasion to say that all the plans and proceedings of the Society have met my approbation; and I assert that it has never done a single act with which any political party or the people of any section of the country can justly find fault. The name of its President, Mr. Brown, of Providence, and of its Treasurer, Mr. Lawrence, of Boston, are a sufficient guaranty in the estimation of intelligent men against its being engaged in any fanatical enterprise. Its stockholders are composed of men of all political parties except Abolitionists. I am not aware that it has received the patronage of that class of our fellow-citizens, and I am informed that some of them disapprove of its proceedings."

The acts of the Company have been such as might be expected from auspices thus severely careful at all points. The secret, through which, with small means, it has been able to accomplish so much, is, that, *as an inducement to emigration, it has gone forward and planted capital in advance of population.* According to the old immethodical system, this rule is reversed, and population has been left to grope blindly, without the advantage of fixed centres, with mills, schools, and churches—all calculated to soften the hardships of pioneer life—such as have been established beforehand in Kansas. Here, sir, is the secret of the Emigrant Aid Company. By this single principle, which is now practically applied for the first time in history, and which has the simplicity of genius, a business association at a distance, without a large capital, has become a beneficent instrument of civilization, exercising the functions of various Societies, and in itself being a Missionary Society, a Bible Society, a Tract Society, an Education Society, and a Society for the Diffusion of the Mechanic Arts. I would not claim too much for this Company; but I doubt if, at this moment, there is any Society, which is so completely philanthropic; and since its leading idea, like the light of a candle from which other candles are lighted without number, may be applied indefinitely, it promises to be an important aid to Human Progress. The lesson it teaches cannot be forgotten, and hereafter, wherever unsettled lands exist, intelligent capital will lead the way, anticipating the wants of the pioneer—nay, doing the very work of the original pioneer—while, amidst well-arranged harmonies, a new community will arise, to become, by its example, a more eloquent preacher than any solitary missionary. In subordination to this essential idea, is its humbler machinery for the aid of emigrants on their way, by combining parties, so that friends and neighbors might journey together; by purchasing tickets at wholesale, and furnishing them to individuals at the actual cost; by providing for each party a conductor familiar with the road, and, through these simple means, promoting the economy, safety, and comfort, of the expedition. The number of emigrants it has directly aided, even thus slightly, in their journey, has been infinitely exaggerated. From the beginning of its operations down to the close of the last autumn, all its detachments from Massachusetts contained only thirteen hundred and twelve persons.

Such is the simple tale of the Emigrant Aid Company. Sir, not even suspicion can justly touch it. But it must be made a scapegoat. This is the decree which has gone forth. I was hardly surprised at this outrage, when it proceeded from the President, for, like Macbeth, he is stepped so far in, that returning were as tedious as go on; but I did not expect it from the Senator from Missouri, [Mr. GEYER,] whom I had learned to respect for the general moderation of his views, and the name he has won in an honorable profession. Listening to him, I was saddened by the spectacle of the extent to which Slavery will sway a candid mind to do injustice. Had any other interest been in question, that Senator would have scorned to join in impeachment of such an association. His instincts as a lawyer, as a man of honor, and as a Senator, would have forbidden; but the Slave Power, in enforcing its behests, allows no hesitation, and the Senator surrendered.

In this vindication, I content myself with a statement of facts, rather than an argument. It might be urged that Missouri had organized a propagandist emigration long before any from Massachusetts, and you might be reminded of the wolf in the fable, which complained of the lamb for disturbing the waters, when in fact the alleged offender was lower down on the stream. It might be urged, also, that South Carolina has lately entered upon a similar system—while one of her chieftains, in rallying recruits, has unconsciously attested to the cause in which he was engaged, by exclaiming, in the words of Satan, addressed to his wicked forces, "Awake! arise! or be forever fallen!" * But the occasion needs no such defences. I put them aside. Not on the example of Missouri or the example of South Carolina, but on inherent rights, which no man, whether Senator or President, can justly assail, do I plant this impregnable justification. It will not do, in specious phrases, to allege the right of every State to be free in its domestic policy from foreign interference, and then to assume such wrongful interference by this Company. By the law and Constitution, we stand or fall; and that law and Constitution we have in no respect offended.

To cloak the overthrow of all law in Kansas, an assumption is now set up, which utterly denies one of the plainest rights of the people everywhere. Sir, I beg Senators to understand that this is a Government of laws; and that, under these laws, the people have an incontestable right to settle any portion of our broad territory, and, if they choose, to propagate any opinions there, not openly forbidden by the laws. If this were not so, pray, sir, by what title is the Senator from Illinois, who is an emigrant from Vermont, propagating his disastrous opinions in another State? Surely he has no monopoly of this right. Others may do what he is doing; nor can the right be in any way restrained. It is as broad as the people; and it matters not whether they go in numbers small or great, with assistance or

---

* Mr. EVANS, of South Carolina, here interrupted Mr. SUMNER to say that he did not know of any such address. Mr. S. replied, that it was taken from Southern papers.

without assistance, under the auspices of societies or not under such auspices. If this were not so, then, by what title are so many foreigners annually naturalized, under Democratic auspices, in order to secure their votes for misnamed Democratic principles? And if capital as well as combination cannot be employed, by what title do venerable associations exist, of ampler means and longer duration than any Emigrant Aid Company, around which cluster the regard and confidence of the country—the Tract Society, a powerful corporation, which scatters its publications freely in every corner of the land—the Bible Society, an incorporated body, with large resources, which seeks to carry the Book of Life alike into Territories and States—the Missionary Society, also an incorporated body, with large resources, which sends its agents everywhere, at home and in foreign lands? By what title do all these exist? Nay, sir, by what title does an Insurance Company in New York send its agent to open an office in New Orleans, and by what title does Massachusetts capital contribute to the Hannibal and St. Joseph Railroad in Missouri, and also to the copper mines of Michigan? The Senator inveighs against the Native American party; but his own principle is narrower than any attributed to them. They object to the influence of emigrants from abroad; he objects to the influence of American citizens at home, when exerted in States or Territories where they were not born! The whole assumption is too audacious for respectful argument. But since a great right has been denied, the children of the Free States, over whose cradles has shone the North Star, owe it to themselves, to their ancestors, and to Freedom itself, that this right should now be asserted to the fullest extent. By the blessing of God, and under the continued protection of the laws, they will go to Kansas, there to plant their homes, in the hope of elevating this Territory soon into the sisterhood of Free States; and to such end they will not hesitate, in the employment of all legitimate means, whether by companies of men or contributions of money, to swell a virtuous emigration, and they will justly scout any attempt to question this unquestionable right. Sir, if they failed to do this, they would be fit only for slaves themselves.

God be praised! Massachusetts, honored Commonwealth that gives me the privilege to plead for Kansas on this floor, knows her rights, and will maintain them firmly to the end. This is not the first time in history, that her public acts have been arraigned, and that her public men have been exposed to contumely. Thus was it when, in the olden time, she began the great battle whose fruits you all enjoy. But never yet has she occupied a position so lofty as at this hour. By the intelligence of her population—by the resources of her industry—by her commerce, cleaving every wave—by her manufactures, various as human skill—by her institutions of education, various as human knowledge—by her institutions of benevolence, various as human suffering—by the pages of her scholars and historians—by the voices of her poets and orators, she is now exerting an influence more subtle and commanding than ever before—shooting her far-darting rays wherever ignorance, wretchedness, or wrong, prevail, and flashing light even upon those who travel far to persecute her. Such is Massachusetts, and I am proud to believe that you may as well attempt, with puny arm, to topple down the earth-rooted, heaven-kissing granite which crowns the historic sod of Bunker Hill, as to change her fixed resolves for Freedom everywhere, and especially now for Freedom in Kansas. I exult, too, that in this battle, which surpasses far in moral grandeur the whole war of the Revolution, she is able to preserve her just eminence. To the first she contributed a larger number of troops than any other State in the Union, and larger than all the Slave States together; and now to the second, which is not of contending armies, but of contending opinions, on whose issue hangs trembling the advancing civilization of the country, she contributes, through the manifold and endless intellectual activity of her children, more of that divine spark by which opinions are quickened into life, than is contributed by any other State, or by all the Slave States together, while her annual productive industry excels in value three times the whole vaunted cotton crop of the whole South.

Sir, to men on earth it belongs only to deserve success; not to secure it; and I know not how soon the efforts of Massachusetts will wear the crown of triumph. But it cannot be that she acts wrong for herself or children, when in this cause she thus encounters reproach. No; by the generous souls who were exposed at Lexington; by those who stood arrayed at Bunker Hill; by the many from her bosom who, on all the fields of the first great struggle, lent their vigorous arms to the cause of all; by the children she has borne, whose names alone are national trophies, is Massachusetts now vowed irrevocably to this work. What belongs to the faithful servant she will do in all things, and Providence shall determine the result.

And here ends what I have to say of the four Apologies for the Crime against Kansas.

III. From this ample survey, where one obstruction after another has been removed, I now pass, in the third place, to the consideration of the *various remedies proposed*, ending with the TRUE REMEDY.

The Remedy should be co-extensive with the original Wrong; and since, by the passage of the Nebraska Bill, not only Kansas, but also Nebraska, Minnesota, Washington, and even Oregon, have been opened to Slavery, the original Prohibition should be restored to its complete activity throughout these various Territories. By such a happy restoration, made in good faith, the whole country would be replaced in the condition which it enjoyed before the introduction of that dishonest measure. Here is the Alpha and the Omega of our aim in this immediate controversy. But no such extensive measure is now in question. The Crime against Kansas has been special, and all else is absorbed in the special remedies for it. Of these I shall now speak.

As the Apologies were four-fold, so are the

Remedies proposed four-fold, and they range themselves in natural order, under designations which so truly disclose their character as even to supersede argument. First, we have the Remedy of Tyranny; next, the Remedy of Folly; next, the Remedy of Injustice and Civil War; and fourthly, the Remedy of Justice and Peace. There are the four caskets; and you are to determine which shall be opened by Senatorial votes.

There is the *Remedy of Tyranny*, which, like its complement, the Apology of Tyranny—though espoused on this floor, especially by the Senator from Illinois—proceeds from the President, and is embodied in a special message. It proposes to enforce obedience to the existing laws of Kansas, "whether Federal or *local*," when, in fact, Kansas has no "local" laws except those imposed by the Usurpation from Missouri, and it calls for additional appropriations to complete this work of tyranny.

I shall not follow the President in his elaborate endeavor to prejudge the contested election now pending in the House of Representatives; for this whole matter belongs to the privileges of that body, and neither the President nor the Senate has a right to intermeddle therewith. I do not touch it. But now, while dismissing it, I should not pardon myself, if I failed to add, that any person who founds his claim to a seat in Congress on the pretended votes of hirelings from another State, with no home on the soil of Kansas, plays the part of Anacharsis Clootz, who, at the bar of the French Convention, undertook to represent nations that knew him not, or, if they knew him, scorned him; with this difference, that in our American case, the excessive farce of the transaction cannot cover its tragedy. But all this I put aside—to deal only with what is legitimately before the Senate.

I expose simply the Tyranny which upholds the existing Usurpation, and asks for additional appropriations. Let it be judged by an example, from which in this country there can be no appeal. Here is the speech of George III, made from the Throne to Parliament, in response to the complaints of the Province of Massachusetts Bay, which, though smarting under laws passed by usurped power, had yet avoided all armed opposition, while Lexington and Bunker Hill still slumbered in rural solitude, unconscious of the historic kindred which they were soon to claim. Instead of Massachusetts Bay, in the Royal speech, substitute Kansas, and the message of the President will be found fresh on the lips of the British King. Listen now to the words, which, in opening Parliament, 30th November, 1774, his Majesty, according to the official report, was pleased to speak:

"*My Lords and Gentlemen:*

"It gives me much concern that I am obliged, at the opening of this Parliament, to inform you that a most daring *spirit of resistance and disobedience to the law* still unhappily prevails in the Province of the *Massachusetts Bay*, and has in divers parts of it broke forth in fresh violences of a very criminal nature. *These proceedings have been countenanced in other of my Colonies*, and *unwarrantable attempts have been made to obstruct the Commerce of this Kingdom, by unlawful combinations.* I have taken such measures and given such orders as I have judged most proper and effectual *for carrying into execution the laws which were passed in the last session of the late Parliament*, for the protection and security of the Commerce of my subjects, and for the restoring and preserving peace, order, and good government, in the Province of the *Massachusetts Bay*."—*American Archives*, 4th series, vol. 1, page 1465.

The King complained of a "daring spirit of resistance and disobedience to the law;" so also does the President. The King adds, that it has "broke forth in fresh violences of a very criminal nature;" so also does the President. The King declares that these proceedings have been "countenanced and encouraged in other of my Colonies;" even so the President declares that Kansas has found sympathy in "remote States." The King inveighs against "unwarrantable measures" and "unlawful combinations;" even so inveighs the President. The King proclaims that he has taken the necessary steps "for carrying into execution the laws," passed in defiance of the constitutional rights of the Colonies; even so the President proclaims that he shall "exert the whole power of the Federal Executive" to support the Usurpation in Kansas. The parallel is complete. The Message, if not copied from the Speech of the King, has been fashioned on the same original block, and must be dismissed to the same limbo. I dismiss its tyrannical assumptions in favor of the Usurpation. I dismiss also its petition for additional appropriations in the affected desire to maintain order in Kansas. It is not money or troops that you need there; but simply the good will of the President. That is all, absolutely. Let his complicity with the Crime cease, and peace will be restored. For myself, I will not consent to wad the National artillery with fresh appropriation bills, when its murderous hail is to be directed against the constitutional rights of my fellow-citizens.

Next comes the *Remedy of Folly*, which, indeed, is also a Remedy of Tyranny; but its Folly is so surpassing as to eclipse even its Tyranny. It does not proceed from the President. With this proposition he is not in any way chargeable. It comes from the Senator from South Carolina, who, at the close of a long speech, offered it as his single contribution to the adjustment of this question, and who thus far stands alone in its support. It might, therefore, fitly bear his name; but that which I now give to it is a more suggestive synonym.

This proposition, nakedly expressed, is that the people of Kansas should be deprived of their arms. That I may not do the least injustice to the Senator, I quote his precise words:

"The President of the United States is under the highest and most solemn obligations to interpose; and if I were to indicate the manner in which he should interpose in Kansas, I would point out the old common law process. I would serve a warrant on Sharpe's rifles, and if Sharpe's rifles did not answer the summons, and come into court on a day certain, or if they resisted the sheriff, I would summon the *posse comitatus*, and would have Colonel Sumner's regiment to be a part of that *posse comitatus*."

Really, sir, has it come to this? The rifle has ever been the companion of the pioneer, and, under God, his tutelary protector against the red man and the beast of the forest. Never was this efficient weapon more needed in just self-defence, than now in Kansas, and at least one article in our National Constitution must be blotted out, before the complete right to it can in any way be impeached. And yet such is the madness of the hour, that, in defiance of the solemn guaranty, embodied in the Amendments to the Constitution, that "the right of the people to keep and bear arms shall not be infringed," the people of Kansas have been arraigned for keeping and bearing them, and the Senator from South Carolina has had the face to say openly, on this floor, that they should be disarmed—of course, that the fanatics of Slavery, his allies and constituents, may meet no impediment. Sir, the Senator is venerable with years; he is reputed also to have worn at home, in the State which he represents, judicial honors; and he is placed here at the head of an important Committee occupied particularly with questions of law; but neither his years, nor his position, past or present, can give respectability to the demand he has made, or save him from indignant condemnation, when, to compass the wretched purposes of a wretched cause, he thus proposes to trample on one of the plainest provisions of constitutional liberty.

Next comes the *Remedy of Injustice and Civil War*—organized by Act of Congress. This proposition, which is also an offshoot of the original Remedy of Tyranny, proceeds from the Senator from Illinois, [Mr. DOUGLAS,] with the sanction of the Committee on Territories, and is embodied in the Bill which is now pressed to a vote.

By this Bill it is proposed, as follows:

"That whenever it shall appear, by a census to be taken under the direction of the Governor, by the authority of the Legislature, that there shall be 93,420 inhabitants (that being the number required by the present ratio of representation for a member of Congress) within the limits hereafter described as the Territory of Kansas, *the Legislature of said Territory shall be, and is hereby, authorized to provide by law for the election of delegates*, by the people of said Territory, to assemble in Convention and form a Constitution and State Government, preparatory, to their admission into the Union on an equal footing with the original States in all respects whatsoever, by the name of the State of Kansas."

Now, sir, consider these words carefully, and you will see that, however plausible and velvet-pawed they may seem, yet in reality they are most unjust and cruel. While affecting to initiate honest proceedings for the formation of a State, they furnish to this Territory no redress for the Crime under which it suffers; nay, they recognise the very Usurpation, in which the Crime ended, and proceed to endow it with new prerogatives. It is *by the authority of the Legislature* that the census is to be taken, which is the first step in the work. It is also *by the authority of the Legislature* that a Convention is to be called for the formation of a Constitution, which is the second step. But the Legislature is not obliged to take either of these steps. To its absolute wilfulness is it left to act or not to act in the premises. And since, in the ordinary course of business, there can be no action of the Legislature till January of the next year, all these steps, which are preliminary in their character, are postponed till after that distant day—thus keeping this great question open, to distract and irritate the country. Clearly this is not what is required. The country desires peace at once, and is determined to have it. But this objection is slight by the side of the glaring Tyranny, that, in recognising the Legislature, and conferring upon it these new powers, the Bill recognises the existing Usurpation, not only as the authentic Government of the Territory for the time being, but also as possessing a creative power to reproduce itself in the new State. Pass this Bill, and you enlist Congress in the conspiracy, not only to keep the people of Kansas in their present subjugation, throughout their Territorial existence, but also to protract this subjugation into their existence as a State, while you legalize and perpetuate the very *force* by which Slavery has been already planted there.

I know that there is another deceptive clause, which seems to throw certain safeguards around the election of delegates to the Convention, *when that Convention shall be ordered by the Legislature*; but out of this very clause do I draw a condemnation of the Usurpation which the Bill recognises. It provides that the tests, coupled with the electoral franchise, shall not prevail in the election of delegates, and thus impliedly condemns them. But if they are not to prevail on this occasion, why are they permitted at the election of the Legislature? If they are unjust in the one case, they are unjust in the other. If annulled at the election of delegates, they should be annulled at the election of the Legislature; *whereas the Bill of the Senator leaves all these offensive tests in full activity at the election of the very Legislature out of which this whole proceeding is to come*, and it leaves the polls at both elections in the control of the officers appointed by the Usurpation. Consider well the facts. By an existing statute, establishing the Fugitive Slave Bill as a shibboleth, a large portion of the honest citizens are excluded from voting for the Legislature, while, by another statute, all who present themselves with a fee of one dollar, whether from Missouri or not, and who can utter this shibboleth, are entitled to vote. And it is a Legislature thus chosen, under the auspices of officers appointed by the Usurpation, that you now propose to invest with parental powers to rear the Territory into a State. You recognise and confirm the Usurpation, which you ought to annul without delay. You put the infant State, now preparing to take a place in our sisterhood, to suckle with the wolf, which you ought at once to kill. The improbable story of Baron Münchausen is verified. The bear, which thrust itself into the harness of the horse it had devoured, and then whirled the sledge according to mere brutal bent, is recognised by this bill, and kept in its usurped place, when the safety of all requires that it should be shot.

In characterizing this Bill as the Remedy of Injustice and Civil War, I give it a plain, self-evident title. It is a continuation of the Crime against Kansas, and as such deserves the same condemnation. It can only be defended by those who defend the Crime. Sir, you cannot expect that the people of Kansas will submit to the Usurpation which this bill sets up, and bids them bow before—as the Austrian tyrant set up his cap in the Swiss market-place. If you madly persevere, Kansas will not be without her William Tell, who will refuse at all hazards to recognise the tyrannical edict; and this will be the beginning of civil war.

Next, and lastly, comes the *Remedy of Justice and Peace*, proposed by the Senator from New York, [Mr. SEWARD,] and embodied in his Bill for the immediate admission of Kansas as a State of this Union, now pending as a substitute for the bill of the Senator from Illinois. This is sustained by the prayer of the people of the Territory, setting forth a Constitution formed by a spontaneous movement, in which all there had opportunity to participate, without distinction of party. Rarely has any proposition, so simple in character, so entirely practicable, so absolutely within your power, been presented, which promised at once such beneficent results. In its adoption, the Crime against Kansas will be all happily absolved, the Usurpation which it established will be peacefully suppressed, and order will be permanently secured. By a joyful metamorphosis, this fair Territory may be saved from outrage.

> "Oh help," she cries, "in this extremest need,
> If you who hear are Deities indeed;
> Gape earth, and make for this dread foe a tomb
> *Or change my form, whence all my sorrows come."*

In offering this proposition, the Senator from New York has entitled himself to the gratitude of the country. He has, throughout a life of unsurpassed industry, and of eminent ability, done much for Freedom, which the world will not let die; but he has done nothing more opportune than this, and he has uttered no words more effective than the speech, so masterly and ingenious, by which he has vindicated it.

Kansas now presents herself for admission with a Constitution republican in form. And, independent of the great necessity of the case, three considerations of fact concur in commending her. First. She thus testifies her willingness to relieve the Federal Government of the considerable pecuniary responsibility to which it is now exposed on account of the pretended Territorial Government. Secondly. She has by her recent conduct, particularly in repelling the invasion at Wakarusa, evinced an ability to defend her Government. And, thirdly, by the pecuniary credit, which she now enjoys, she shows an undoubted ability to support it. What now can stand in her way?

The power of Congress to admit Kansas at once is explicit. It is found in a single clause of the Constitution, which, standing by itself, without any qualification applicable to the present case, and without doubtful words, requires no commentary. Here it is:

> "New States *may* be admitted by Congress into this Union; but no new State shall be formed or erected within the jurisdiction of any other State, nor any State be formed by the junction of two or more States or parts of States, without the consent of the Legislatures of the States concerned, as well as of the Congress."

New States MAY be admitted. Out of that little word, *may*, comes the power, broadly and fully—without any limitation founded on population or preliminary forms—provided the State is not within the jurisdiction of another State, nor formed by the junction of two or more States or parts of States, without the consent of the Legislatures of the States. Kansas is not within the *legal* jurisdiction of another State, although the laws of Missouri have been tyrannically extended over her; nor is Kansas formed by the junction of two or more States; and, therefore, Kansas *may* be admitted by Congress into the Union, without regard to population or preliminary forms. You cannot deny the power, without obliterating this clause of the Constitution. The Senator from New York was right in rejecting all appeal to precedents, as entirely irrelevant; for the power invoked is clear and express in the Constitution, which is above all precedent. But, since precedent has been enlisted, let us look at precedent.

It is objected that the *population* of Kansas is not sufficient for a State; and this objection is sustained by under-reckoning the numbers there, and exaggerating the numbers required by precedent. In the absence of any recent census, it is impossible to do more than approximate to the actual population; but, from careful inquiry of the best sources, I am led to place it now at 50,000, though I observe that a prudent authority, the *Boston Daily Advertiser*, puts it as high as 60,000, and, while I speak, this remarkable population, fed by fresh emigration, is outstripping even these calculations. Nor can there be a doubt, that, before the assent of Congress can be perfected in the ordinary course of legislation, this population will swell to the large number of 93,420, required in the Bill of the Senator from Illinois. *But, in making this number the condition of the admission of Kansas, you set up an extraordinary standard.* There is nothing out of which it can be derived, from the beginning to the end of the precedents. Going back to the days of the Continental Congress, you will find that, in 1784, it was declared that 20,000 freemen in a Territory might "establish a permanent Constitution and Government for themselves," (*Journals of Congress, Vol. 4, p. 379*;) and, though this number was afterwards, in the Ordinance of 1787 for the Northwestern Territory, raised to 60,000, yet the power was left in Congress, and subsequently exercised in more than one instance, to constitute a State with a smaller number. Out of all the new States, only Maine, Wisconsin, and Texas, contained, at the time of their admission into the Union, so large a population as it is proposed to require in Kansas; while no less than *fourteen* new States have been admitted with a smaller population; as will appear in the following list, which is the result of research, showing the number of "free inhabitants" in these States at the time of the proceedings which ended in their admission:

Vermont	- - 85,416	Illinois -	- - 45,000
Kentucky	- - 61,103	Missouri	- - 56,586
Tennessee	- - 66,649	Arkansas	- - 41,000
Ohio -	- - 50,000	Michigan	- - 92,673
Louisiana	- - 41,890	Florida -	- - 27,091
Indiana -	- - 60,000	Iowa -	- - 81,921
Mississippi	- - 35,000	California	- - 92,597
Alabama	- - 50,000		

But this is not all. At the adoption of the Federal Constitution, there were three of the old Thirteen States whose respective populations did not reach the amount now required for Kansas. These were Delaware, with a population of 59,096; Rhode Island, with a population of 64,689; and Georgia, with a population of 82,548. And even now, while I speak, there are at least two States, with Senators on this floor, which, according to the last census, do not contain the population now required of Kansas. I refer to Delaware, with a population of 91,635, and Florida, with a population of freemen amounting only to 47,203. So much for precedents of population.

But in sustaining this objection, it is not uncommon to depart from the strict rule of numerical precedent, by suggesting that the population required in a new State has always been, in point of fact, above the existing ratio of representation for a member of the House of Representatives. But this is not true; for at least one State, Florida, was admitted with a population below this ratio, which at the time was 70,680. So much, again, for precedents. But even if this coincidence were complete, it would be impossible to press it into a binding precedent. The rule seems reasonable, and, in ordinary cases, would not be questioned; but it cannot be drawn or implied from the Constitution. Besides, this ratio is, in itself, a sliding scale. At first, it was 33,000, and thus continued till 1811, when it was put at 35,000. In 1822, it was 40,000; in 1832, it was 47,700; in 1842, it was 70,680; and now, it is 93,420. If any ratio is to be made the foundation of a binding rule, it should be that which prevailed at the adoption of the Constitution, and which still continued when Kansas, as a part of Louisiana, was acquired from France, under solemn stipulation that it should "be incorporated into the Union of the United States *as soon as* may be consistent with the principles of the Federal Constitution." But this whole objection is met by the memorial of the people of Florida, which, if good for that State, is also good for Kansas. Here is a passage:

"But the people of Florida respectfully insist that their right to be admitted into the Federal Union as a State is not dependent upon the fact of their having a population equal to such ratio. Their right to admission, it is conceived, is guarantied by the express pledge in the sixth article of the treaty before quoted; and if any rule as to the number of the population is to govern, it should be that in existence at the time of the cession, which was thirty-five thousand. They submit, however, that any ratio of representation, dependent upon legislative action, based solely on convenience and expediency, shifting and vacillating as the opinion of a majority of Congress may make it, now greater than at a previous apportionment, but which a future Congress may prescribe to be less, cannot be one of the *constitutional* "PRINCIPLES" referred to in the treaty, consistency with which, by its terms, is required. It is, in truth, but a mere regulation, not founded on principle. No specified number of population is required by any recognised principle as necessary in the establishment of a free Government.

"It is in no wise '*inconsistent with the principles of the Federal Constitution*,' that the population of a State should be less than the ratio of Congressional representation. The very case is provided for in the Constitution. With such deficient population, she would be entitled to one Representative. If any event should cause a decrease of the population of one of the States even to a number below the *minimum* ratio of representation prescribed by the Constitution, she would still remain a member of the Confederacy, and be entitled to such Representative. It is respectfully urged, that a rule or principle which would not justify the *expulsion* of a State with a deficient population, on the ground of inconsistency with the Constitution, should not exclude or prohibit *admission*."—(*Exec. Doc., 27th Cong., 2d sess., Vol. 4, No. 206.*)

Thus, sir, do the people of Florida plead for the people of Kansas.

Distrusting the objection from inadequacy of population, it is said that the *proceedings for the formation of a new State are fatally defective in form*. It is not asserted that a previous enabling Act of Congress is indispensable; for there are notorious precedents the other way, among which are Kentucky in 1791; Tennessee in 1796; Maine in 1820; and Arkansas and Michigan in 1836. But it is urged that in no instance has a State been admitted, whose Constitution was formed without such enabling Act, or without the authority of the Territorial Legislature. This is not true; for California came into the Union with a Constitution, formed not only without any previous enabling Act, but also without any sanction from a Territorial Legislature. The proceedings which ended in this Constitution were initiated by the military Governor there, acting under the exigency of the hour. This instance may not be identical in all respects with that of Kansas; but it displaces completely one of the assumptions which Kansas now encounters, and it also shows completely the disposition to relax all rule, under the exigency of the hour, in order to do substantial justice.

But there is a memorable instance, which contains in itself every element of irregularity which you denounce in the proceedings of Kansas. Michigan, now cherished with such pride as a sister State, achieved admission into the Union in persistent defiance of all rule. Do you ask for precedents? Here is a precedent for the largest latitude, which you, who profess a deference to precedent, cannot disown. Mark now the stages of this case. The first proceedings of Michigan were without any previous enabling Act of Congress; and she presented herself at your door with a Constitution thus formed, and with Senators chosen under that Constitution—precisely as Kansas now. This was in December, 1835, while Andrew Jackson was President. By the leaders of the Democracy at that time, all objection for alleged defects of form was scouted, and language was employed which is strictly applicable to Kansas. There is nothing new under the sun; and the very objection of the President, that the application of Kansas proceeds from "persons acting against authorities duly constituted by Act of Congress," was hurled against the application of Michigan, in debate on this floor, by Mr. Hendricks, of Indiana. This was his language:

"But the people of Michigan, in presenting their Senate and House of Representatives as the legislative power existing there, *showed that they had trampled upon and violated the laws of the United States establishing a Territorial Government in Michigan*. These laws were, or ought to be, in full force there; but, by the character and position assumed, they had set up a Government antagonist to that of the United States."—(*Congress. Deb., Vol. 12, p. 236, 24th Cong., 1st session.*)

To this impeachment Mr. Benton replied in these effective words:

"Conventions were original acts of the people. They depended upon inherent and inalienable rights. The people of any State may at any time meet in Convention, without a law of their Legislature, and without any provision, or against any provision in their Constitution, and may alter or abolish the whole frame of Government as they please. The sovereign power to govern themselves was in the majority, and they could not be divested of it."—(*Ibid.*, p. 1036.)

Mr. Buchanan vied with Mr. Benton in vindicating the new State:

"The precedent in the case of Tennessee has completely silenced all opposition in regard to the necessity of a previous act of Congress to enable the people of Michigan to form a State Constitution. It now seems to be conceded that our subsequent approbation is equivalent to our previous action. This can no longer be doubted. *We have the unquestionable power of waiving any irregularities in the mode of framing the Constitution, had any such existed*"—(*Ibid.*, p. 1041.)

"He did hope that by this bill all objections would be removed; and that this State, so ready to rush into our arms, would not be repulsed, *because of the absence of some formalities which perhaps were very proper, but certainly not indispensable.*"—(*Ibid.*, p. 1015.)

After an animated contest in the Senate, the Bill for the admission of Michigan, *on her assent to certain conditions*, was passed, by 23 yeas to 8 nays. But you find weight, as well as numbers, on the side of the new State. Among the yeas were Thomas H. Benton of Missouri, James Buchanan of Pennsylvania, Silas Wright of New York, W. R. King of Alabama.—(*Cong. Globe, Vol. 3d, p.* 276, *1st session 24th Cong.*) Subsequently, on motion of Mr. Buchanan, the two gentlemen sent as Senators by the new State received the regular compensation for attendance throughout the very session in which their seats had been so acrimoniously assailed.—(*Ibid., p.* 448.)

In the House of Representatives the application was equally successful. The Committee, on the Judiciary, in an elaborate report, reviewed the objections, and, among other things, said:

"That the people of Michigan have, without due authority, formed a State Government, but, nevertheless, *that Congress has power to waive any objection which might, on that account, be entertained* to the ratification of the Constitution which they have adopted, and to admit their Senators and Representatives to take their seats in the Congress of the United States."—(*Exec. Doc*, *1st sess. 24th Cong.*, *Vol.* 2, *No* 380.)

The House sustained this view by a vote of 153 yeas to 45 nays. In this large majority, by which the title of Michigan was then recognised, will be found the name of Franklin Pierce, at that time a Representative from New Hampshire.

But the case was not ended. The fiercest trial and the greatest irregularity remained. The Act providing for the admission of the new State contained a modification of its boundaries, and proceeded to require, as a *fundamental condition*, that these should "receive the assent of a Convention of delegates, elected by the people of the said State, for the sole purpose of giving the assent herein required."—(*Statutes at Large, Vol.* 5, *p.* 50, *Act of June 5th*, 1836.) Such a Convention, duly elected under a call from the Legislature, met in pursuance of law, and, after consideration, declined to come into the Union on the condition proposed. But the action of this Convention was not universally satisfactory, and in order to effect an admission into the Union, another Convention was called *professedly* by the people, in their sovereign capacity, without any authority from State or Territorial Legislature; nay, sir, according to the language of the present President, "against authorities duly constituted by Act of Congress;" at least as much as the recent Convention in Kansas. The irregularity of this Convention was increased by the circumstance, that two of the oldest counties of the State, comprising a population of some 25,000 souls, refused to take any part in it, even to the extent of not opening the polls for the election of delegates, claiming that it was held without warrant of law, and in defiance of the legal Convention. This popular Convention, though wanting a popular support co-extensive with the State, yet proceeded, by formal act, to give the assent of the people of Michigan to the fundamental condition proposed by Congress.

The proceedings of the two Conventions were transmitted to President Jackson, who, by message, dated 27th December, 1836, laid them both before Congress, indicating very clearly his desire to ascertain the will of the people, without regard to form. The origin of the popular Convention he thus describes:

"This Convention was not held or elected by virtue of any act of the Territorial or State Legislature. It originated from the People themselves, and was chosen by them in pursuance of resolutions adopted in primary assemblies held in the respective counties."—(*Sen. Doc.*, *2d sess. 24th Cong.*, *Vol.* 1, *No.* 36.)

And he then declares that, had these proceedings come to him during the recess of Congress, he should have felt it his duty, on being satisfied that they emanated from a Convention of delegates elected *in point of fact by the People of the State*, to issue his proclamation for the admission of the State.

The Committee on the Judiciary in the Senate, of which Felix Grundy was Chairman, after inquiry, recognised the competency of the popular Convention, as "elected by the People of the State of Michigan," and reported a Bill, responsive to their assent of the proposed condition, for the admission of the State without further condition.—(*Statutes at Large, Vol.* 5, *p.* 144, *Act of 26th Jan.*, 1837.) Then, sir, appeared the very objections which are now directed against Kansas. It was complained that the movement for immediate admission was the work of "a minority," and that "a great majority of the State feel otherwise."—(*Sen. Doc.*, *2d sess. 24th Cong.*, *Vol.* 1, *No.* 37.) And a leading Senator, of great ability and integrity, Mr. Ewing, of Ohio, broke forth in a catechism which would do for the present hour. He exclaimed:

"What evidence had the Senate of the organization of the Convention? Of the organization of the popular assemblies who appointed their delegates to that Convention? None on earth. Who they were that met and voted, we had no information. Who gave the notice? And for what did the People receive the notice? To meet and elect? What evidence was there that the Convention acted according to law? Were the delegates sworn? And, if so, they were extra-judicial oaths, and not binding upon them. Were the votes counted? In fact, it was not a proceeding under the forms of law, for they were totally disregarded."—(*Cong. Globe*, *Vol.* 4, *p.* 60, *2d sess. 24th Cong.*)

And the same able Senator, on another occasion, after exposing the imperfect evidence with regard to the action of the Convention, existing only in letters and in an article from a Detroit newspaper, again exclaimed:

> "This, sir, is the evidence to support an organic law of a new State about to enter into the Union! Yes, of an organic law, the very highest act a community of men can perform. Letters referring to other letters and a scrap of a newspaper."—(*Cong. Debates, Vol.* 13, *Part I, p.* 233.)

It was Mr. Calhoun, however, who pressed the opposition with the most persevering intensity. In his sight, the admission of Michigan, under the circumstances, "would be the most monstrous proceeding under our Constitution that can be conceived, the most repugnant to its principles and dangerous in its consequences."—(*Cong. Debates, Vol.* 13, *p.* 210.) "There is not," he exclaimed, "one particle of official evidence before us. We have nothing but the private letters of individuals, who do not know even the numbers that voted on either occasion. They know nothing of the qualifications of voters, nor how their votes were received, nor by whom counted."—(*Ibid.*) And he proceeded to characterize the popular Convention as "not only a party caucus, for party purpose, but a criminal meeting—a meeting to subvert the authority of the State and to assume its sovereignty"—adding, "that the actors in that meeting might be indicted, tried, and punished"—and he expressed astonishment that "a self-created meeting, convened for a criminal object, had dared to present to this Government an act of theirs, and to expect that we are to receive this irregular and criminal act as a fulfilment of the condition which we had presented for the admission of the State!"—(*Ibid., p.* 299.) No stronger words have been employed against Kansas.

But the single question on which all the proceedings then hinged, and which is as pertinent in the case of Kansas as in the case of Michigan, was thus put by Mr. MORRIS, of Ohio—(*Ibid, p.* 215)—"*Will Congress recognise as valid, constitutional, and obligatory, without the color of a law of Michigan to sustain it, an act done by the People of that State in their primary assemblies, and acknowledge that act as obligatory on the constituted authorities and Legislature of the State?*" This question, thus distinctly presented, was answered in debate by able Senators, among whom were Mr. BENTON and Mr. KING. But there was one person, who has since enjoyed much public confidence, and has left many memorials of an industrious career in the Senate and in diplomatic life, JAMES BUCHANAN, who rendered himself conspicuous by the ability and ardor with which, against all assaults, he upheld the cause of the popular Convention, which was so strongly denounced, and the entire conformity of its proceedings with the genius of American Institutions. His speeches on that occasion contain an unanswerable argument, at all points, *mutato nomine*, for the immediate admission of Kansas under her present Constitution; nor is there anything by which he is now distinguished that will redound so truly to his fame—if he only continues true to them. But the question was emphatically answered in the Senate by the final vote on the passage of the Bill, where we find 25 yeas to only 10 nays. In the House of Representatives, after debate, the question was answered in the same way, by a vote of 148 yeas to 58 nays; and among the yeas is again the name of FRANKLIN PIERCE, a Representative from New Hampshire.

Thus, in that day, by such triumphant votes, did the cause of Kansas prevail in the name of Michigan. A popular Convention—called absolutely without authority, and containing delegates from a portion only of the population—called, too, in opposition to constituted authorities, and in derogation of another Convention assembled under the forms of law—stigmatized as a caucus and a criminal meeting, whose authors were liable to indictment, trial, and punishment—was, after ample debate, recognised by Congress as valid, and Michigan now holds her place in the Union, and her Senators sit on this floor, by virtue of that act. Sir, if Michigan is legitimate, Kansas cannot be illegitimate. You bastardize Michigan when you refuse to recognise Kansas.

Again, I say, do you require a precedent? I give it to you. But I will not stake this cause on any precedent. I plant it firmly on the fundamental principle of American Institutions, as embodied in the Declaration of Independence, by which Government is recognised as deriving its just powers only *from the consent of the governed*, who may alter or abolish it when it becomes destructive of their rights. In the debate on the Nebraska Bill, at the overthrow of the Prohibition of Slavery, the Declaration of Independence was denounced as a "self-evident lie." It is only by a similar audacity that the fundamental principle, which sustains the proceedings in Kansas, can be assailed. Nay, more: you must disown the Declaration of Independence, and adopt the Circular of the Holy Alliance, which declares that "useful and necessary changes in legislation and in the administration of States *ought only to emanate from the free will and the intelligent and well-weighed conviction of those whom God has rendered responsible for power.*" Face to face, I put the principle of the Declaration of Independence and the principle of the Holy Alliance, and bid them grapple! "The one places the remedy in the hands which *feel* the disorder; the other places the remedy in the hands which *cause* the disorder;" and when I thus truthfully characterize them, I but adopt a sententious phrase from the Debates in the Virginia Convention on the adoption of the Federal Constitution.—(3 *Elliot's Debates*, 107—*Mr. Corbin.*) And now these two principles, embodied in the rival propositions of the Senator from New York and the Senator from Illinois, must grapple on this floor.

Statesmen and judges, publicists and authors, with names of authority in American history, espouse and vindicate the American principle. Hand in hand, they now stand around Kansas, and feel this new State lean on them for support. Of these I content myself with adducing two only, both from slaveholding Virginia, in days when Human Rights were not without support in that State. Listen to the language of St. George Tucker, the distinguished commentator upon Blackstone, uttered from the bench in a judicial opinion:

"The power of convening the legal Assemblies, or the ordinary constitutional Legislature, *resided solely in the Executive.* They could neither be chosen without writs issued by its authority, nor assemble, when chosen, but under the same authority. The Conventions, on the contrary, were chosen and assembled, either in pursuance of recommendations from Congress, or from their own bodies, *or by the discretion and common consent of the people.* They were held even whilst a legal Assembly existed. Witness the Convention held at Richmond, in March, 1775; after which period, the legal constitutional Assembly was convened in Williamsburg, by the Governor, Lord Dunmore. * * * *Yet a constitutional dependence on the British Government was never denied until the succeeding May.* * * The Convention, then, was not the ordinary Legislature of Virginia. It was the body of the people, impelled to assemble from a sense of common danger, consulting for the common good, and acting in all things for the common safety."—(1 *Virginia Cases*, 70, 71, *Kamper vs. Hawkins.*)

Listen also to the language of James Madison:

"That in all great changes of established government, forms ought to give way to substance; that a rigid adherence in such cases to the forms would render nominal and nugatory the transcendent and precious right of the people 'to abolish or alter their Government, as to them shall seem most likely to effect their safety and happiness.' * * Nor can it have been forgotten *that no little ill-timed scruples, no zeal for adhering to ordinary forms, were anywhere seen, except in those who wished to indulge under these masks their secret enmity to the substance contended for.*"—(*The Federalist*, No. 40.)

Proceedings thus sustained, I am unwilling to call *revolutionary*, although this term has the sanction of the Senator from New York. They are founded on an unquestionable American right, declared with Independence, confirmed by the blood of the fathers, and expounded by patriots, which cannot be impeached without impairing the liberties of all. On this head the language of Mr. Buchanan, in reply to Mr. Calhoun, is explicit:

"Does the Senator [Mr. Calhoun] contend, then, that if, in one of the States of this Union, the Government be so organized as to utterly destroy the right of equal representation, there is no mode of obtaining redress, but by an act of the Legislature authorizing a Convention, or by open rebellion? Must the people step at once from oppression to open war? Must it be either absolute submission, or absolute revolution? *Is there no middle course?* I cannot agree with the Senator. I say that the whole history of our Government establishes the principle that the people are sovereign, and that a majority of them can alter or change their fundamental laws at pleasure. *I deny that this is either rebellion or revolution. It is an essential and a recognised principle in all our forms of government.*"—(*Congress. Deb., Vol. 13, p. 313, 24th Cong., 2d session.*)

Surely, sir, if ever there was occasion for the exercise of this right, the time had come in Kansas. The people there had been subjugated by a horde of foreign invaders, and brought under a tyrannical code of revolting barbarity, while property and life among them were left exposed to audacious assaults which flaunted at noonday, and to reptile abuses which crawled in the darkness of night. *Self-defence is the first law of nature;* and unless this law is temporarily silenced—as all other law has been silenced there—you cannot condemn the proceedings in Kansas. Here, sir, is an unquestionable authority—*in itself an overwhelming law*—which belongs to all countries and times—which is the same in Kansas as at Athens and Rome—which is now, and will be hereafter, as it was in other days—in presence of which Acts of Congress and Constitutions are powerless, as the voice of man against the thunder which rolls through the sky—which whispers itself coeval with life—whose very breath is life itself; and now, in the last resort, do I place all these proceedings under this supreme safeguard, which you will assail in vain. Any opposition must be founded on a fundamental perversion of facts, or a perversion of fundamental principles, which no speeches can uphold, though surpassing in numbers the nine hundred thousand piles driven into the mud in order to sustain the Dutch Stad-house at Amsterdam!

Thus, on every ground of precedent, whether as regards population or forms of proceeding; also, on the vital principle of American Institutions; and, lastly, on the absolute law of self-defence, do I now invoke the power of Congress to admit Kansas at once and without hesitation into the Union. "New States *may* be admitted by the Congress into the Union;" such are the words of the Constitution. If you hesitate for want of precedent, then do I appeal to the great principle of American Institutions. If, forgetting the origin of the Republic, you turn away from this principle, then, in the name of human nature, trampled down and oppressed, but aroused to a just self-defence, do I plead for the exercise of this power. Do not hearken, I pray you, to the propositions of Tyranny and Folly; do not be ensnared by that other proposition of the Senator from Illinois, [Mr. DOUGLAS,] in which is the horrid root of Injustice and Civil War. But apply gladly, and at once, the True Remedy, wherein are Justice and Peace.

Mr. President, an immense space has been traversed, and I now stand at the goal. The argument in its various parts is here closed. The Crime against Kansas has been displayed in its origin and extent, beginning with the overthrow of the Prohibition of Slavery; next cropping out in conspiracy on the borders of Missouri; then hardening into a continuity of outrage, through organized invasions and miscellaneous assaults, in which all security was destroyed, and ending at last in the perfect subjugation of a generous people to an unprecedented Usurpation. Turning aghast from the Crime, which, like murder, seemed to confess itself "with most miraculous organ," we have looked with mingled shame and indignation upon the four Apologies, whether of Tyranny, Imbecility, Absurdity, or Infamy, in which it has been wrapped, marking especially the false testimony, congenial with the original Crime, against the Emigrant Aid Company. Then were noted, in succession, the four Remedies, whether of Tyranny—Folly—Injustice and Civil War—or Justice and Peace, which last bids Kansas, in conformity with past precedents and under the exigencies of the hour, in order to redeem her from Usurpation, to take a place as a sovereign State of the Union; and this is the True Remedy. If in this argument I have not unworthily vindicated Truth, then have I spoken according to my desires; if imperfectly, then only according to my powers. But there are other things, not belonging to the argument, which still press for utterance.

Sir, the people of Kansas, bone of your bone and flesh of your flesh, with the education of freemen and the rights of American citizens, now stand at your door. Will you send them away, or bid them enter? Will you push them back to renew their struggles with a deadly foe, or will you preserve them in security and peace? Will you cast them again into the den of Tyranny, or will you help their despairing efforts to escape? These questions I put with no common solicitude; for I feel that on their just determination depend all the most precious interests of the Republic; and I perceive too clearly the prejudices in the way, and the accumulating bitterness against this distant people, now claiming their simple birthright, while I am bowed with mortification, as I recognise the President of the United States, who should have been a staff to the weak and a shield to the innocent, at the head of this strange oppression.

At every stage, the similitude between the wrongs of Kansas, and those other wrongs against which our fathers rose, becomes more apparent. Read the Declaration of Independence, and there is hardly an accusation which is there directed against the British Monarch, which may not now be directed with increased force against the American President. The parallel has a fearful particularity. Our fathers complained that the King had "sent hither swarms of officers, to harass our people, and eat out their substance;" that he "had combined, with others, to subject us to a jurisdiction foreign to our Constitution, *giving his assent to their acts of pretended legislation;*" that "he had abdicated government here, by declaring us out of his protection, and *waging war against us;*" that "he had excited domestic insurrection among us, and *endeavored to bring on the inhabitants of our frontier the merciless savages;*" that "our repeated petitions have been answered only by repeated injury." And this arraignment was aptly followed by the damning words, that "a Prince, whose character is thus marked by every act which may define a tyrant, is unfit to be the ruler of a free people." And surely, a President who has done all these things, cannot be less unfit than a Prince. At every stage, the responsibility is brought directly to him. His offence has been both of commission and omission. He has done that which he ought not to have done, and he has left undone that which he ought to have done. By his activity the Prohibition of Slavery was overturned. By his failure to act, the honest emigrants in Kansas have been left a prey to wrong of all kinds. *Nullum flagitium extitit, nisi per te; nullum flagitium sine te.* And now he stands forth the most conspicuous enemy of that unhappy Territory.

As the tyranny of the British King is all renewed in the President, so on this floor have the old indignities been renewed, which embittered and fomented the troubles of our Fathers. The early petition of the American Congress to Parliament, long before any suggestion of Independence, was opposed — like the petitions of Kansas — because that body "was assembled without any requisition on the part of the Supreme Power." Another petition from New York, presented by Edmund Burke, was flatly rejected, as claiming rights derogatory to Parliament. And still another petition from Massachusetts Bay was dismissed as "vexatious and scandalous," while the patriot philosopher who bore it was exposed to peculiar contumely. Throughout the debates, our fathers were made the butt of sorry jests and supercilious assumptions. And now these scenes with these precise objections, have been renewed in the American Senate.

With regret, I come again upon the Senator from South Carolina, [Mr. BUTLER,] who, omnipresent in this debate, overflowed with rage at the simple suggestion that Kansas had applied for admission as a State; and, with incoherent phrases, discharged the loose expectoration of his speech, now upon her representative, and then upon her people. There was no extravagance of the ancient Parliamentary debate which he did not repeat; nor was there any possible deviation from truth which he did not make, with so much of passion, I am glad to add, as to save him from the suspicion of intentional aberration. But the Senator touches nothing which he does not disfigure—with error, sometimes of principle, sometimes of fact. He shows an incapacity of accuracy, whether in stating the Constitution or in stating the law, whether in the details of statistics or the diversions of scholarship. He cannot ope his mouth, but out there flies a blunder. Surely he ought to be familiar with the life of Franklin; and yet he referred to this household character, while acting as agent of our fathers in England, as above suspicion; and this was done that he might give point to a false contrast with the agent of Kansas—not knowing that, however they may differ in genius and fame, in this experience they are alike: that Franklin, when intrusted with the petition of Massachusetts Bay, was assaulted by a foul-mouthed speaker, where he could not be heard in defence, and denounced as a "thief," even as the agent of Kansas has been assaulted on this floor, and denounced as a "forger." And let not the vanity of the Senator be inspired by the parallel with the British statesmen of that day; for it is only in hostility to Freedom that any parallel can be recognised.

But it is against the people of Kansas that the sensibilities of the Senator are particularly aroused. Coming, as he announces, "from a State"—aye, sir, from South Carolina—he turns with lordly disgust from this newly-formed community, which he will not recognise even as "a body politic." Pray, sir, by what title does he indulge in this egotism? Has he read the history of "the State" which he represents? He cannot surely have forgotten its shameful imbecility from Slavery, confessed throughout the Revolution, followed by its more shameful assumptions for Slavery since. He cannot have forgotten its wretched persistence in the slave trade as the very apple of its eye, and the condition of its participation in the Union. He cannot have forgotten its Constitution, which is republican only in name, confirming power in the hands of the few, and founding the qualifications of its legislators on "a settled freehold estate and ten negroes." And yet the Senator, to whom that "State" has in part committed the guardianship of its good name, instead of moving, with backward treading steps, to cover its nakedness, rushes forward, in the very ecstacy of madness, to expose it, by provoking a comparison with Kansas. South Carolina is old; Kansas is young. South Carolina counts by centuries, where Kansas counts by years. But a beneficent example may be born in a day; and I venture to say, that against the two centuries of the older "State," may be already set the two years of trial, evolving corresponding virtue, in the younger community. In the one, is the long wail of Slavery; in the other, the hymns of Freedom. And if we glance at special achievements, it will be difficult to find anything in the history of South Carolina which presents so much of heroic spirit in an heroic cause as appears in that repulse of the Missouri invaders by the beleaguered town of Lawrence, where even the women gave their effective efforts to Freedom. The matrons of Rome, who poured their jewels into the treasury for the public defence—the wives of Prussia, who, with delicate fingers, clothed their defenders against French invasion—the mothers of our own Revolution, who sent forth their sons, covered over with prayers and blessings, to combat for Human Rights, did nothing of self-sacrifice truer than did these women on this occasion. Were the whole history of South Carolina blotted out of existence, from its very beginning down to the day of the last election of the Senator to his present seat on this floor, civilization might lose—I do not say how little; but surely less than it has already gained by the example of Kansas, in its valiant struggle against oppression, and in the development of a new science of emigration. Already in Lawrence alone there are newspapers and schools, including a High School, and throughout this infant Territory there is more of mature scholarship, in proportion to its inhabitants, than in all South Carolina. Ah, sir, I tell the Senator that Kansas, welcomed as a Free State, will be a "ministering angel" to the Republic, when South Carolina, in the cloak of darkness which she hugs, "lies howling."

The Senator from Illinois [MR. DOUGLAS] naturally joins the Senator from South Carolina in this warfare, and gives to it the superior intensity of his nature. He thinks that the National Government has not completely proved its power, as it has never hanged a traitor; but, if the occasion requires, he hopes there will be no hesitation; and this threat is directed at Kansas, and even at the friends of Kansas throughout the country. Again occurs the parallel with the struggles of our Fathers, and I borrow the language of Patrick Henry, when, to the cry from the Senator, of "treason," "treason," I reply, "if this be treason, make the most of it." Sir, it is easy to call names; but I beg to tell the Senator that if the word "traitor" is in any way applicable to those who refuse submission to a tyrannical Usurpation, whether in Kansas or elsewhere, then must some new word, of deeper color, be invented, to designate those mad spirits who would endanger and degrade the Republic, while they betray all the cherished sentiments of the Fathers and the spirit of the Constitution, in order to give new spread to Slavery. Let the Senator proceed. It will not be the first time in history, that a scaffold erected for punishment has become a pedestal of honor. Out of death comes life, and the "traitor" whom he blindly executes will live immortal in the cause.

For Humanity sweeps onward; where to-day the martyr stands,
On the morrow crouches Judas, with the silver in his hands;
While the hooting mob of yesterday in silent awe return,
To glean up the scattered ashes into History's golden urn.

Among these hostile Senators, there is yet another, with all the prejudices of the Senator from South Carolina, but without his generous impulses, who, on account of his character before the country, and the rancor of his opposition, deserves to be named. I mean the Senator from Virginia, [MR. MASON,] who, as the author of the Fugitive Slave Bill, has associated himself with a special act of inhumanity and tyranny. Of him I shall say little, for he has said little in this debate, though within that little was compressed the bitterness of a life absorbed in the support of Slavery. He holds the commission of Virginia; but he does not represent that early Virginia, so dear to our hearts, which gave to us the pen of Jefferson, by which the equality of men was declared, and the sword of Washington, by which Independence was secured; but he represents that other Virginia, from which Washington and Jefferson now avert their faces, where human beings are bred as cattle for the shambles, and where a dungeon rewards the pious matron who teaches little children to relieve their bondage by reading the Book of Life. It is proper that such a Senator, representing such a State, should rail against Free Kansas.

But this is not all. The precedent is still more clinching. Thus far I have followed exclusively the public documents laid before Congress, and illustrated by the debates of that body; but well-authenticated facts, not of record here, make the case stronger still. It is sometimes said that the proceedings in Kansas are defective, because they originated in a party. This is not true; but even if it were true, then would they still find support in the example of Michigan, where all the proceedings, stretching through successive years, began and ended in party. The proposed State Government was pressed by the Democrats as a *party test;* and all who did not embark in it were denounced. Of the Legislative Council, which called the first Constitutional Convention in 1835, all were Democrats; and in the Convention itself, composed of eighty-seven members, only seven were Whigs. The Convention of 1836, which gave the final assent, originated in a Democratic Convention on the 29th October, in the county of Wayne, composed of one hundred and twenty-four delegates, all Democrats, who proceeded to resolve—

"That the delegates of the *Democratic party* of Wayne, solemnly impressed with the spreading evils and dangers which a refusal to go into the Union has brought upon the people of Michigan, earnestly recommend meetings to be immediately convened by their fellow-citizens in every county of the State, with a view to the expression of their sentiments in favor of the election and call of another

Convention, in time to secure our admission into the Union before the first of January next."

Shortly afterwards, a committee of five, appointed by this Convention, all leading Democrats, issued a circular, "under the authority of the delegates of the county of Wayne," recommending that the voters throughout Michigan should meet and elect delegates to a Convention to give the necessary assent to the Act of Congress. In pursuance of this call, the Convention met; and, as it originated in an exclusively party recommendation, so it was of an exclusively party character. And it was the action of this Convention that was submitted to Congress, and, after discussion in both bodies, on solemn votes, approved.

But the precedent of Michigan has another feature, which is entitled to the gravest attention, especially at this moment, when citizens engaged in the effort to establish a State Government in Kansas are openly arrested on the charge of treason, and we are startled by tidings of the maddest efforts to press this procedure of preposterous Tyranny. No such madness prevailed under Andrew Jackson; although, during the long pendency of the Michigan proceedings, for more than fourteen months, the Territorial Government was entirely ousted, and the State Government organized in all its departments. One hundred and thirty different legislative acts were passed, providing for elections, imposing taxes, erecting corporations, and establishing courts of justice, including a Supreme Court and a Court of Chancery. All process was issued in the name of the people of the State of Michigan. And yet no attempt was made to question the legal validity of these proceedings, whether legislative or judicial. Least of all did any menial Governor, dressed in a little brief authority, play the fantastic tricks which we now witness in Kansas; nor did any person, wearing the robes of justice, shock high Heaven with the mockery of injustice now enacted by emissaries of the President in that Territory. No, sir; nothing of this kind then occurred. Andrew Jackson was President.

Senators such as these are the natural enemies of Kansas, and I introduce them with reluctance, simply that the country may understand the character of the hostility which must be overcome. Arrayed with them, of course, are all who unite, under any pretext or apology, in the propagandism of Human Slavery. To such, indeed, the time-honored safeguards of popular rights can be a name only, and nothing more. What are trial by jury, habeas corpus, the ballot-box, the right of petition, the liberty of Kansas, your liberty, sir, or mine, to one who lends himself, not merely to the support at home, but to the propagandism abroad, of that preposterous wrong, which denies even the right of a man to himself! Such a cause can be maintained only by a practical subversion of all rights. It is, therefore, merely according to reason that its partisans should uphold the Usurpation in Kansas.

To overthrow this Usurpation is now the special, importunate duty of Congress, admitting of no hesitation or postponement. To this end it must lift itself from the cabals of candidates, the machinations of party, and the low level of vulgar strife. It must turn from that Slave Oligarchy which now controls the Republic, and refuse to be its tool. Let its power be stretched forth towards this distant Territory, not to bind, but to unbind; not for the oppression of the weak, but for the subversion of the tyrannical; not for the prop and maintenance of a revolting Usurpation, but for the confirmation of Liberty.

These are imperial arts, and worthy thee!

Let it now take its stand between the living and dead, and cause this plague to be stayed. All this it can do; and if the interests of Slavery did not oppose, all this it would do at once, in reverent regard for justice, law, and order, driving far away all the alarms of war; nor would it dare to brave the shame and punishment of this Great Refusal. But the Slave Power dares anything; and it can be conquered only by the united masses of the People. From Congress to the People, I appeal.

Already Public Opinion gathers unwonted forces to scourge the aggressors. In the press, in daily conversation, wherever two or three are gathered together, there the indignant utterance finds vent. And trade, by unerring indications, attests the growing energy. Public credit in Missouri droops. The six per cents of that State, which at par should be 102, have sunk to 84¼—thus at once completing the evidence of Crime, and attesting its punishment. Business is now turning from the Assassins and Thugs, that infest the Missouri River on the way to Kansas, to seek some safer avenue. And this, though not unimportant in itself, is typical of greater changes. The political credit of the men who uphold the Usurpation, droops even more than the stocks; and the People are turning from all those through whom the Assassins and Thugs have derived their disgraceful immunity.

It was said of old, "Cursed be he that removeth his neighbor's Landmark. *And all the people shall say, Amen.*"—(*Deut.* xxvii, 17.) Cursed, it is said, in the city, and in the field; cursed in basket and store; cursed when thou comest in, and cursed when thou goest out. These are terrible imprecations; but if ever any Landmark were sacred, it was that by which an immense territory was guarded *forever* against Slavery; and if ever such imprecations could justly descend upon any one, they must descend now upon all who, not content with the removal of this sacred Landmark, have since, with criminal complicity, fostered the incursions of the great Wrong against which it was intended to guard. But I utter no imprecations. These are not my words; nor is it my part to add to or subtract from them. But thanks be to God! they find a response in the hearts of an aroused People, making them turn from every man, whether President, or Senator, or Representative, who has been engaged in this Crime—especially from those who, cradled in free institutions, are without the apology of education or social prejudice—until of all such those other words of the prophet shall be fulfilled—"I will set my face against that man, and make him a sign and a proverb, and I will cut him him off from the midst of my people."—(*Ezekiel* xiv, 8.)

Turning thus from the authors of this Crime, the People will unite once more with the Fathers of the Republic, in a just condemnation of Slavery—determined especially that it shall find no home in the National Territories — while the Slave Power, in which the Crime had its beginning, and by which it is now sustained, will be swept into the charnel-house of defunct Tyrannies.

In this contest, Kansas bravely stands forth—the stripling leader, clad in the panoply of American institutions. In calmly meeting and adopting a frame of Government, her people have with intuitive promptitude performed the duties of freemen; and when I consider the difficulties by which she was beset, I find dignity in her attitude. *In offering herself for admission into the Union as a* FREE STATE, *she presents a single issue for the people to decide.* And since the Slave Power now stakes on this issue all its ill-gotten supremacy, the People, while vindicating Kansas, will at the same time overthrow this Tyranny. Thus does the contest which she now begins involve not only Liberty for herself, but for the whole country. God be praised, that she did not bend ignobly beneath the yoke! Far away on the prairies, she is now battling for the Liberty of all, against the President, who misrepresents all. Everywhere among those who are not insensible to Right, the generous struggle meets a generous response. From innumerable throbbing hearts go forth the very words of encouragement which, in the sorrowful days of our Fathers, were sent by Virginia, speaking by the pen of Richard Henry Lee, to Massachusetts, in the person of her popular tribune, Samuel Adams:

"CHANTILLY, VA., *June* 23, 1774.

"I hope the good people of Boston will not lose their spirits under their present heavy oppression, for they will certainly be supported by the other Colonies; and the cause for which they suffer is so glorious and so deeply interesting to the present and future generations, that all America will owe, in a great measure, their political salvation to the present virtue of Massachusetts Bay."—(*American Archives, 4th series, Vol. 1, p.* 446.)

In all this sympathy there is strength. But in the cause itself there is angelic power. Unseen of men, the great spirits of History combat by the side of the people of Kansas, breathing a divine courage. Above all towers the majestic form of Washington once more, as on the bloody field, bidding them to remember those rights of Human Nature for which the War of Independence was waged. Such a cause, thus sustained, is invincible.

The contest, which, beginning in Kansas, has reached us, will soon be transferred from Congress to a broader stage, where every citizen will be not only spectator, but actor; and to their judgment I confidently appeal. To the People, now on the eve of exercising the electoral franchise, in choosing a Chief Magistrate of the Republic, I appeal, to vindicate the electoral franchise in Kansas. Let the ballot-box of the Union, with multitudinous might, protect the ballot-box in that Territory. Let the voters everywhere, while rejoicing in their own rights, help to guard the equal rights of distant fellow-citizens; that the shrines of popular institutions, now desecrated, may be sanctified anew; that the ballot-box, now plundered, may be restored; and that the cry, "I am an American citizen," may not be sent forth in vain against outrage of every kind. In just regard for free labor in that Territory, which it is sought to blast by unwelcome association with slave labor; in Christian sympathy with the slave, whom it is proposed to task and to sell there; in stern condemnation of the Crime which has been consummated on that beautiful soil; in rescue of fellow-citizens, now subjugated to a tyrannical Usurpation; in dutiful respect for the early Fathers, whose aspirations are now ignobly thwarted; in the name of the Constitution, which has been outraged—of the Laws trampled down—of Justice banished—of Humanity degraded—of Peace destroyed—of Freedom crushed to earth; and, in the name of the Heavenly Father, whose service is perfect Freedom, I make this last appeal.

GEO. S. BLANCHARD,
Publisher, Bookseller, and Stationer,
39 WEST FOURTH STREET, CINCINNATI.

DIARY AND CORRESPONDENCE
OF THE LATE
AMOS LAWRENCE,
EDITED BY HIS SON, WILLIAM R. LAWRENCE, M.D.

With elegant Steel Portraits of Amos and Abbott Lawrence, and other Illustrations.

Royal 12mo., Cloth. Price $1.00.

The octavo edition of this Work has had an almost unexampled sale. Within six months after the first publication of this Work, *twenty-two thousand* copies had been sold. This extraordinary sale is to be accounted for by the character of the Man, and the merits of the Book. It is the Memoir of a Boston Merchant, who became distinguished for his great wealth, but more distinguished for the manner in which he used it. It is the Memoir of a man, who, commencing business with only twenty dollars, gave away in public and private charities, *during his life time*, more than **SEVEN HUNDRED THOUSAND DOLLARS.**

As a book for young men, it has been pronounced invaluable. In this conviction, merchants and business men have largely purchased it for presents to their clerks and employees. In Boston more than

EIGHTY MERCANTILE HOUSES

Have thus put upon it the stamp of their approval; in some cases one hundred copies; in others fifty, forty, twenty-five, fifteen, &c., having been purchased by a single firm. This example has been followed in New York, Philadelphia and other places.

CLERGYMEN regarding the Book as a rare means of healthful influence in the community, have voluntarily contributed to extend its circulation, by making it the basis of sermons and lectures, and recommending it in public assemblies.

The New York *Independent* volunteers this emphatic commendation of the Work. "We are proud of this Book. We are willing to let it go forth to other lands as a specimen of what America can produce. The good effect which this Life may have in determining the course of young men to honor and virtue is incalculable."

So high is the estimation put upon the Book in all quarters, that urgent and repeated demands have been made upon the publishers, by the press and by individuals, for a cheaper edition, notwithstanding the price of the octavo edition is much below what is usually charged for such a volume. Yielding to this demand they now offer to the public a

CHEAP EDITION.

It is a large 12mo. volume, printed on thick, white paper, from the plates of the octavo edition, and is sold at the extremely low price of One Dollar. All things considered, the publisher is confident that a cheaper book will not be found in the market.

Copies sent by mail, POSTAGE PAID, on the receipt of the price of the book.

KNOWLEDGE IS POWER,

A View of the Productive Forces of Modern Society, and the Results of Labor, Capital & Skill.

BY CHARLES KNIGHT.

CONTAINING OVER FIFTY ENGRAVINGS. PRICE, **$1.25.**

The demand for this valuable work, which commenced even before its publication, is constantly increasing. All who have read the Book agree in pronouncing it a work of *unquestioned merit.* It is elegantly written, is of a popular character, and is peculiary fitted, as well as designed to entertain, inform, and instruct the million. A glance at any page will be sufficient to convince the reader of this.

"One of the ablest, and in many respects, the most remarkable Book of the Day. No person who desires to be familiar with modern improvements, should neglect it. It contains the recorded footprints of mind in its onward march; the "route book" of practical thought; the "log" of the "run" investigation is making in every department of business."—*Athenæum.*

Copies sent by mail, POST PAID, on the receipt of the price of the book.

GEO S. BLANCHARD, Publisher,

39 West Fourth Street, Cincinnati.

www.ingramcontent.com/pod-product-compliance
Lightning Source LLC
LaVergne TN
LVHW011127110826
845150LV00008B/2267

* 9 7 8 1 4 1 8 1 9 4 7 4 1 *